The Long Goodbye

a true story of abandonment

MARIA PARK

Author's Note

Writing *The Long Goodbye* has been a deeply cathartic experience for me, though not without its moments of emotional upheaval. I remember one evening, sitting in my caravan, deciding to read a random passage aloud to my son. I had always been composed while writing, so I didn't think much of it, until I got three lines in and broke down sobbing. It was unexpected and overwhelming, but maybe it was a sign that I hadn't been dealing with everything as well as I thought. Or perhaps it was just a wobble.

This book poured out of me faster than I imagined, just three weeks to reach a first draft, and once I started, I couldn't stop. It was almost addictive, perhaps because I've been carrying this story inside me for so long. Finally putting it into words was both a release and a challenge.

Do I feel relieved now that it's written? It's too early to tell. But am I glad it's out? Absolutely. This story had to be told, and I hope I've done it justice. I've never done anything like this before, and I likely never will again, but I've done my best to tell the full truth.

If you notice a name has been changed - or left out entirely - that was deliberate. Some people deserved the respect of anonymity, while others didn't deserve the privilege of being part of my story.

Above all, I wrote this book to help others understand what being abandoned truly feels like. It's not just about the pain of being left behind; it's also about the hope that one day you'll be rescued, a hope that can become as toxic as the abandonment itself. My greatest wish is that this story reaches those who need to hear it, offering them clarity, validation, or simply the knowledge that they are not alone.

Thank you for joining me on this journey.

Maria Park

Contents

Hamilton Home

I never really had a permanent home. I was too young to understand the reasons back then, but looking back, it was obvious that we were always on the edge of something collapsing. Our mother, Katie, had a way of burning through every chance she got, whether it was with her drinking or the company she kept.

One day when I was two years old, we were packed up and told we were going somewhere new, as if it was the most normal thing in the world. That 'somewhere' ended up being Hamilton Home, the place that was supposed to take care of us when Katie couldn't. We arrived with nothing but a few bags and each other. That's how we ended up there, four kids, our mother, and the promise of something better, which never came.

Hamilton Home, my first adventure into the care system, all because we were homeless thanks to Katie's fondness for 'wreck the hoose juice', the vilest lager I've ever tried. You would need to be an alcoholic to drink the stuff, but it did the trick for her, and within three cans of the 9% vol lager, she would either be fighting with someone or leading the Salvation Army band up the road.

You could never tell how her mood would be from one hour to the next. It really all depended on what can she was on, or how many she had left. She was a violent drunk as well, to anyone who crossed her: men, women, children, or even animals.

The idea of 'home' was never something that stayed the same for long. From a very early age, it was clear that the places where I stayed weren't homes, not in the way most people thought of them. And perhaps it's fitting that Hamilton Home, looked nothing like the warm, safe place a home was supposed to be. It was large and depressing, inside and out. A Victorian mansion made of sandstone that was probably a nice shade of cream when it was built, but when we were there, it all looked black, even the large wall that ran the length of the building was as dark as two in the morning.

I didn't mind too much; I had all my family around me, my alcoholic mother, Katie, and my siblings - my older sister Sarah, and my brothers Roddy and Dunky. Dunky was my oldest brother and my absolute hero - if it wasn't for his tenacious manner, we might well have starved to death. I would have done anything for Dunky, and he for me.

I found out from my social work file that we were at Hamilton Home twice; we left the first time because of a drunk woman who was causing all sorts of grief. I find it really funny that Katie was objecting to a drunk woman. Maybe she saw herself in the woman and didn't like what she had seen.

The second time we left was because I was sexually assaulted by the home's handyman. He was the vilest wee man you could ever meet. He had a hump on his back that made him look like a camel. He always wore the same old tatty suit jacket that stank to the heavens.

Up until that day, I was happy-go-lucky, small for my age yet a normal wee girl - but that man changed my whole world that morning, and for the rest of my life. I never managed to regain my confident, independent way again.

I had been out exploring the home by myself, as everyone else was asleep. What started out as a lovely day with the sun out turned into a horror story. As I got to the gable end of the home (which I had just found out led to the kitchens), I saw *The Hump*. He was over in the corner with his stinking suit jacket on. He asked me to come over, and like a trusting innocent, I went.

3

As soon as I was within arm's reach, he grabbed me close to him and then proceeded to put what felt like his whole hand inside me while he rubbed his privates hard against me.

I knew instantly I had to get myself away from him, so I struggled free and took off like the devil was after me. I never stopped, not even for a second. I just knew I had to get to safety, and that lay in the arms of Dunky.

I made it to the dormitory we were all housed in and found Katie and Dunky. I told them through tears of distress what had just occurred with The Hump. All I know is they left that dorm in a mad hurry, I'm sure to give The Hump the kicking of his life. That's how things got sorted in our world.

I wish he had been charged, as I'm sure he was part of a paedophile ring. I say that because I found out a long time later that he had been put out of a relative's house that he was living in because he was caught interfering with their youngest daughter, so he was at it all his life. 'Sick in the head' is the only way to describe him.

We still had no home of our own and would go from drunkard to drunkard, just whoever Katie could talk into allowing five people to stay. Usually, it was only for a night or until the drink ran out. The drink always won!

What happened there, especially the incident with The Hump, left scars that I couldn't just walk away from.

Looking back, it's clear that the system meant to protect us was only the first of many that would fail me. It was also the first time I truly realised how quickly innocence could be taken, and how often the people who were meant to care for us simply turned a blind eye. From that day forward, I knew that trusting anyone again wouldn't come easy.

Leaving Hamilton Home didn't change anything, not really. Each place we went was just another stop on a long road of broken promises. The care system may have given us a roof, but it never gave us what we needed: safety, trust, or stability. Hamilton was only the first in a line of places that taught me how fragile everything could be. We moved from one broken situation to the next, and each time, it chipped away a little more at what was left of me.

Strathaven & Coatshill

After our time at Hamilton Home, life became a blur of faces and places. We drifted from person to person, house to house, clinging to whatever scraps of shelter Katie could wrangle. One night, we ended up with a woman Katie had met at a carry-out shop. She took us back to her home, and for a moment, I thought maybe things would be okay, maybe we'd get a meal, a warm bed, something that felt like care.

However, while Katie and the woman drank in the other room, we were left in the bedroom, forgotten. Hunger gnawed at us like a constant ache, but we didn't dare go to them, not with the smell of alcohol and the sound of laughter sharp and loud on the other side of the door. We knew better than to interrupt.

We were so desperate that we ended up eating salt, pinches of it taken from the edge of a plate. That was our dinner for the night, salt. The taste burned on my tongue, dry and sharp, but it was better than nothing. I can still remember how my stomach twisted in protest, the way the emptiness felt heavier even after we ate.

We even stayed with my grandparents for a while. It was a strange kind of calm, at least compared to what we were used to.

My grandad, Katie's father, who we called Old Donald, once told me that until Katie met my dad, she never touched a drink. I can't see him saying that if it wasn't true, that wasn't his style, as he was a straight-up-and-down guy. He only ever told it how it was. If it's the truth, then my old man has a lot to answer for. I do know he was an alcoholic too, but a functioning one, at least.

Old Donald was a man of few words, but you could always count on him to be straight with you. He didn't sugarcoat things, and I liked that about him. What I did know was that the house always felt a little safer when he was around, even if only for a short time.

Living with them was different from what we had known before. There was always food on the table, and for a little while, we were allowed to just be kids. My siblings and I weren't used to being in one place for too long, and though I didn't realise it then, part of me was always waiting for the next bout of chaos. And of course, it always came.

Katie couldn't stay out of trouble for long. It didn't matter where we went or who we stayed with, she'd always find a way to burn through whatever goodwill people had left. My grandparents were no different. Eventually her drinking and fighting started to wear them down. I could see it in my granny's eyes, the frustration building every time Katie came home in one of her moods, dragging trouble behind her like a shadow.

I remember the last time we stayed with them, the shouting between Katie and my granny echoing through the walls. The words didn't matter. It was always the same argument, different day. My granny had had enough, and I don't blame her. Five extra mouths to feed, with a daughter who couldn't stay sober, it was more than anyone should have to handle.

After we had exhausted all the local drunks and used my granny until she snapped, we went into Strathaven Home, all five of us together. It wasn't a surprise, really. By then, moving felt like part of our routine. Pack what little we had and go. Strathaven was just another place in a long list of homes that never quite felt like home. It was just another stop along the way. We didn't stay long, but it didn't matter - every place started to feel the same after a while. Moving from home to home wasn't unusual for us by then; it was just what we did. The faces changed, the walls changed, but the hunger, the uncertainty, and the fear of what might happen next stayed the same. There was always that feeling in the pit of my stomach that nothing would ever really get better for us.

I don't have many memories of that home; except I thought it was very strange that the dinner hall was a separate portacabin-like structure. It smelled of cabbage anytime I was there. The outskirts of the home were lined with deciduous native trees for as far as you could explore. Roddy loved it there for the trees alone. He was great at climbing anything, and nothing scared him. That's probably why he had broken just about every bone in his body!

After Strathaven Home, we all went straight to Coatshill House in Blantyre. Coatshill was no different from anywhere else we'd been. We stayed there for a while, all five of us crammed into that two-bedroom cottage. It might have been clean, even a bit nicer than the others, but to us, it was just another temporary stop. The only thing that made it different was the secret room behind the couch, a place that, for a little while, made us feel like we had found something special, even if it was just a few hours of escape. That room with its toys and puzzles was a world apart from the reality we were living.

The main home was in front of our cottage. We only ate in there or attended meetings in the main office. The secret room was only opened at night; we were never to go near it during the day. We would move the big heavy three-seater couch to the left, and once we were through the door, it was like a magical fairground had just opened up in front of you.

It had every toy that any kid would ever want. My first glimpse of the secret room was an enormous wooden rocking horse, the real McCoy. It had reins made from real leather, a saddle that looked like something out of a cowboy movie, and metal stirrups , what more could a horse-crazy kid want? I'm sure I got up to 100 MPH on that horse. Well, in my head, I did.

The room had jigsaws galore of every description, from coastal scenes to cottages, all encapsulated in jigsaw form. There were boxes of figures from Spider-Man to Superman and boxes of Barbie dolls and her accessories. My God, I had never imagined it was even possible for a doll to have so much, which probably let me know just how little I had.

I was always suspicious the secret room wasn't actually a real secret, but a way for Katie to lock us all in for a few hours while she visited the nearest pub. Once we went inside, Katie pushed the couch back across the doorway and left us to it. So even if the place caught fire, we could not have escaped, and I'm sure, because it was a completely separate building, nobody would have heard our screams.

No matter how many places we moved to, it was always the same - places that looked like homes but never felt like them. Each new house, each new room, was just another reminder that we didn't really belong anywhere. We were always outsiders, always moving, always waiting for the moment when everything would fall apart again. Looking back, it's hard to remember what was worse: the fear of what might happen or the feeling that nothing ever would.

As we left Coatshill, I started to realise that moving wasn't the hardest part. It was the constant hoping that this time, things would be different. That maybe this place would be the one where everything changed. But it never was.

Each new place brought the same old story, and each move took a little more out of me. By the time we reached Lockview, I had stopped expecting anything at all.

Life in Lockview

The Social Work department portrays our time at Lockview – a block of flats - at 92A Overtown Road - as the most horrific and difficult time of our lives. But I'm sorry, Mr Social Worker, you were so wrong. It was by far the best time of my life.

Wee Streakie was our social worker. He was good at his job as I remember it, and our family certainly put him to the test. I'm sure he would have cringed when he saw our name in the diary for a home visit, especially at Lockview, where Katie would probably present herself drunk and usually very argumentative with him. He was a wee, frail, nearly bald stick of a man, who I'm sure would be unable to stand upright in a bad wind, but he was a real gem of a man to us.

Katie tested his character many a time. Depending on how drunk she was, it would define how their meetings would go. It would usually start off well, then deteriorate quickly as Streakie laid down the law to Katie about how she should be looking after her kids, and that never went down well with her. Trying to reason with a ranting drunk woman who was certain she was right was like hitting a brick wall.

He would usually leave flustered to the bone by Katie and her antics; watching their interactions was better than anything on the TV.

On the day of our arrival at Lockview we had got a bus to the shops at Newmains, all we had to carry were the clothes on our backs. All five of us together, me as happy as a pig in her own muck. It was a really magical day as we wouldn't be homeless anymore. Even the bus ride to our new house felt good.

Once we got off the bus from Glasgow, which we seemed to be on for weeks, we had a long walk to 92A. About halfway, we took some time out, and all five of us sat on a low moss-covered wall for what felt like ages (but I'm sure was only 15 to 20 minutes).

Once we regained our strength to go on, we eventually got to our new abode. (Our joke was that if the police asked for your current address, you would say "No Fixed Abode." And if asked the same, your pal should say "Next door to him!")

Once we got into 92A, we found a bare house. Not a stick of furniture or even a plant pot to be seen, although in a cupboard I found a pile of about forty saucers, every style and design you would ever see or ever want to see.

I found 'Maria's Saucer.' It had a beautiful willow pattern of blue and white, depicting a scene from a tranquil garden someplace in China. That silly saucer meant so much to me once I found it. I was the only one with my own special saucer.

That saucer was very well used, as it became the go-to place for a candle when we ran out of electricity, which was quite often.

After we got to explore the rest of the flat, we all ended up in the kitchen. For some reason, Sarah decided it would be a great idea to turn on the hot water tap, it was attached to its own separate boiler for heating the water. But what Sarah (a true blonde) didn't know at that point was that the hot tap couldn't turn off. So, we had boiling water spewing out the tap for at least three hours until Social Work got a hold of their plumber.

Our Sarah was called every bad name under the sun by Katie after that escapade, which wasn't fair. Sarah wasn't to know it couldn't turn off.

When we went to live at 92A, I hadn't started primary school yet, so I must have only been four years old. Sarah was six, Roddy eight, and Dunky ten, we were obviously a planned family. Our dad was Robert (Rab) Park, a long-distance lorry driver from Airdrie. A happy man, especially if he had a drink in his hand. I have some photos of their wedding day, and he was handsome. Katie was a petite and fresh-faced young woman. Her wedding dress was not like most; it only came to below her knee. Rab had the most polished boots I had ever seen.

I once had the opportunity to ask Rab why he left.

He explained how he was always away from Monday to Friday, driving a long-distance lorry. He would transport all types of produce, from railway sleepers to jars of pickles. I remember the pickles because one Saturday when we were on a visit to his house in Easterhouse, he left me and Dunky at the yard his lorry was stored at, and we found it was loaded with large catering-size jars of pickles. Dunky had the great idea to have a pickle fight. Have you ever been struck by a pickle that's going 50 MPH? I can tell you it stings! When Rab came back and saw the hundreds of pickles all over the yard, he was not a happy man. He was so angry that it took the whole day for him to calm down.

When he would get home on a Friday evening, he would park his lorry at the car park near our house at 5 Queens Crescent. But as time went on, he would come back to find a party in full swing in his house, with every drinker within a two-mile radius in attendance.

The reason Katie became so popular was because of the great wages Rab was making. She could buy drink seven days a week, which made her good for other alcoholics to know.

He was more annoyed about the state of us four kids - dirty, hungry, and living nearly feral - as Katie was always drunk by then. A drunk person can't look after themselves, let alone four kids. Rab said he just couldn't cope with it all, and he left when I was two.

I'd have thought he would stick around and sort it out, as there were four young and vulnerable lives at stake, but that's not how he felt about it.

The chaos of life with Katie, the cold, and the hunger followed us from place to place, but Lockview had its own flavour of disorder. It was the place where drinkers thrived, secrets were kept, and survival meant navigating the unpredictable world of alcohol, gambling, and the constant uncertainty that shaped our everyday lives.

Then there was Harry Daly, or HD as we called him, the man who arrived in our lives out of nowhere, bringing with him a strange mix of comfort and chaos.

Lockview wasn't just a house, it was a world of its own. Katie was always either lost in a haze of alcohol or in the middle of some argument, and HD followed suit. We never knew which version of Katie or HD we'd get:

the ones who could laugh and joke, or the ones who would explode without warning. HD, with his street smarts and clever ways, made life feel less predictable, but that wasn't always a good thing. His love of gambling was just another way to keep us on edge.

It wasn't just the drinking and the fights that filled our days, it was the way the whole place seemed to hum with disorder. Every corner of Lockview had its secrets. The neighbours knew it, and we knew it too. Kids weren't meant to know the things we did, but Lockview had a way of making sure we grew up fast. It was like living in a circus where you never knew if you'd be the performer or the one getting trampled.

One Christmas, Sarah once got a bike from HD but he told her, "Don't go near the bookies with it, I stole it from there."

That was the same year I got my Christmas present in March. Roddy was looking in his wardrobe, the only bit of furniture except a single bed in the whole room, when he came across a brand new three-wheeled plastic tricycle.

"Look what I found," he told Katie.

"OMG!!! That's Maria's Christmas present!" She had been so out of her face on Christmas Eve that she forgot she had got me a present. So, it had lived in that wardrobe until March when Roddy found it along with a police helmet.

I had the best fun with that wee tricycle and the helmet. I was sure I was a real policewoman, I just needed to grow another five feet.

I never did know where HD came from. He just appeared in our life one day and didn't leave. Drinkers attract drinkers, I'm sure it's the same the world over. He was never bad to any of us; I was his favourite by a country mile. I was never far from his coattails, always lurking in the background, watching his every move.

HD was a clever dude, when it came to the ways of the streets, you couldn't teach him much. He had been there, done it, and won the t-shirt!

His two favourite things in the world were drinking and gambling - he was good at both - and he should have been good because he practised plenty.

We had a great dodge to make money; we got copper wire and sold It. We were very fortunate to have the local tip next to our house, a gold mine in our eyes. It was like a one-armed bandit machine that always paid out. As long as I had my trusty pliers, I could make money. Not that I saw much of it.

When I had cut enough cable from kettles, hoovers, and anything electrical we would take it to the scrap man in Cambusnethan. He would exchange our freshly cut cables for cash, so Katie could always afford drink. However, it was only me and HD who went and got cable - Katie never went to the tip - but she was the one enjoying the rewards. I was more than happy about her not coming with us, though. I enjoyed our early morning rambles, just the two of us. The local carry-out shop saw the bulk of the cable money, the bookies got the next chunk, then the kids/house got what was left over, which was never very much.

God only knows what that scrap man thought of HD and me I'd love to meet him again one day and say, "Hey Pal, I turned out good." I once found a pair of Wrangler jeans at the tip which I loved. I wouldn't take them off, even for bed, as I just knew one of my brothers would have been off with them, and I would never have got them back. Eventually, they had to get washed; it was a must. I'm sure they could have stood up on their own accord if left unattended.

HD brought chaos, but in his own strange way, he made things feel less lonely. Even with the constant madness, there were moments when it felt like he was on our side. One of my favourite memories was when HD got lifted by the police. For what, I have no clue.

He came back home that night and asked me if I wanted a puppy.

"Is the Pope a Catholic?" I replied.

What had happened was that while HD was at the custody desk being booked in, a lady came in with a young Alsatian pup she had found wandering along a dual carriageway. Well, HD saw and heard of this, and the next morning, at early bells, him and I walked the four miles to Wishaw police station to declare, "We've lost our Alsatian pup." And that's how easy it was to acquire "Shane," the nicest, most biddable dog you could meet.

Shane was an absolute Alsatian: tan and black, with the Alsatian saddle and the best temperament you could ask for. All a German Shepherd Dog should be (Alsatians and GSD are the same dog).

I really knew I had a good friend when I walked out of that police station that morning with my dog. We had to walk him home on a bit of rope that the nice police lady gave us, as we had no lead. Why would we? We didn't have a dog!

That was the last time Shane was ever on a lead, but he didn't need it, as he never left our side. We would take him anywhere we went. The only thing he hated was Jean Devine's red Boxer dog. It was a vicious brute to both dogs and people, and it once tore Dunky's leg real badly when he forgot that it was tied to the side fence. When he ran to kick a ball, the boxer nailed him until I ran up and gave it an almighty kick to the chin. It let Dunky go, and Roddy pulled him away, but the damage had been done. Dunky was lucky as it could have killed him. Shane never liked that dog, but he had respect for it.

I'm not sure what Shane ate; if we only got the bare minimum. I can't see Katie buying dog food for a dog. She was never an animal lover; she only loved her lagers. It was with glee that she told me, years later, that HD had drowned Shane. I still don't believe that, but maybe that's what he told her.

I was sure she had got rid of him the first morning he came home with us, because we couldn't find him anywhere. Eventually, I did find him, and I was so happy to see his wee cute ears and his big daft puppy feet that looked like they should be on a bigger dog. I didn't let him out of my sight that day. He had been asleep on a pile of clothes inside a dark brown sideboard that stood next to the door. I'm glad Katie couldn't hear the words I was calling her in my head before I found him, or I would have got the kicking of all kickings.

Lockview was unpredictable in every sense, but Shane was my constant. He wasn't just a dog; he was my first real companion, someone who loved me without conditions or judgement. When everything else felt uncertain, Shane was there, trotting beside me with his big puppy feet and warm, trusting eyes. I didn't just care for him, he gave me something to believe in, something good to hold onto.

Shane really was my dog; he adored me and was never far from my side. We spent every second possible together and he ignited my lifelong love of dogs. Even now, I'm known as the woman with the load of dogs. Ask anyone in my village where Maria with the six dogs lives, and they will show you to my house. My love of dogs has stayed with me through every twist and turn my life has taken. Even now, surrounded by my dogs, I think back to him, the first and the best. He got me through those days when it felt like there was little else to rely on, and for that, I'll always be grateful. Shane wasn't just a part of my childhood; he was a part of me.

Lockview was pure chaos, but there were moments when life took a step outside its walls.

Lockview Battles

Lockview had two blocks, our block, which was to the left as you stand in front of it, was known as 'Alkie-traz.' I'm sure I don't need to explain why. The block to the right was full of bought flats and had professional people, like nurses, living there.

A block full of alcoholics and drug users, it doesn't take a lot to start them off, and Katie was usually first in line when it came to an argument. When she was drunk, she was the only one who was right.

I can remember one time while eight months pregnant, Katie, drunk as a skunk, was, for some crazy reason, demanding one of the nice women from the next block come down to the courtyard at the back for her to "knock fuck out of you."

Any self-respecting person would not accept an invite to fight with a drunk woman, let alone a drunk eight-month pregnant lunatic cursing at the very top of her voice. "Come down this stair so I can knock seven colours of shit out of you, ya cow!"

"Mrs Park, I'm not going to fight a pregnant woman."

Katie was having none of that.

Thankfully, the nice lady went indoors and took herself away from the commotion. Katie took that as a win. What a mug! That pregnancy ended in tragedy. She had two stillborn twins.

Lockview was more than just a building, it was its own world, full of strange characters, constant upheaval, and neighbours who seemed as trapped in the chaos as we were. It wasn't a place where you found stability or peace; it was where you learned to live with unpredictability. Every day, something or someone would remind us that life in Lockview had its own rules.

Behind 92A was a large field surrounded by a deep woodland that came out at the coup. I'm so glad to say that place is now a well-looked-after nature reserve - if only it could talk.

Our flat was very small with a sitting room and a kitchen off to the right, the only other thing in the room was a coal fire in front of you as you entered. Along the hallway, you come to the two bedrooms, one straight in front and one to the right. There was the 'big' room where there were two beds; Katie's double behind the door, and a single that Sarah and I used, straight in front of the door. That was all that room had to offer along with a large bay window that looked out at the bing outside. It was a shale hill about half a mile wide, and on the top was a body of water that we called the 'hot water pond'. I am not sure why we called it that, as it was neither hot nor a pond. It was fun to splash around in but it would have taken about 10 minutes to swim from one end to the other.

The other single room had only a single bed, a large dark brown double-door wardrobe, and a single long window. That was it for Dunky and Roddy.

We had a great mix of neighbours in Lockview. The famous singer in Scotland, Sydney Devine, had a sister who lived below us, Jean Devine. She was a drinker, so she fit in well with Katie and HD. She once asked Katie what Dunky needed for starting high school. Katie took great advantage of this and wrote a list as long as her leg. Everything from the blazer to the badge on the blazer, to the tie, to the shoes - anything she could think of got written on that list.

If you're wondering how Jean could afford it all, the truth is she never could. It was all stolen to order, from the tie to the shoes, to the bag, all stolen. From good shops, mind you. Not the usual tat we got from the tip. Dunky looked a class act that first day at Wishaw High. Dapper Dan was his nickname for a while after.

Jean also had a husband, we all called Wee Johnny, a real weasel of a man, all wrinkled, even his ears were creased. He, like the rest of the block, was a heavy drinker.

One time Katie, for some reason, was going to give Roddy a kicking. He was so scared of her that he tipped the large wardrobe against the door so she couldn't get in.

"Move the fucking wardrobe, you wee bastard!"

"No, you're going to batter me!"

"I'm not gonna batter you."

"Aye you are!"

"I'm no, I'm gonna fucking kill you!"

Roddy kept the wardrobe there until she fell into her usual unconscious state later that night.

That was the thing about Lockview, there was never a sense of safety. Even behind locked doors and barricaded wardrobes, the threat was always there, lingering like a shadow over everything we did. Roddy may have kept Katie out that night, but we all knew that the chaos would return. It always did.

Daily Survival

The people, the constant activity, and the wildness of the landscape at Lockview all mirrored the unpredictability of life inside our home. But even in the midst of the confusion, there were moments of freedom, moments when I found ways to entertain myself in the fields and woods, trying to forget the storm that was always waiting at home.

Back home, life was still full of incidents because there was such a variety of people all shoved into two tenement-type blocks of red sandstone that stood alone on a long road with not another house in sight. Surrounded by those trees and fields on all sides, it was a great playground for me. I always had something to get up to when I was the only one at home and the rest were all still at school.

I was usually left to my own ways to entertain myself in the fields behind our flat, or across the road to the bing. Or I could take myself to the tip to look for toys.

Katie's absences weren't new, but every time she left us, it felt like the world got a little smaller. When she was there, she was the centre of everything - good or bad - but when she was gone, we were left to fend for ourselves. Her time in the pubs was just another part of the routine, but for me, it was always about waiting for her to come back, not knowing if she would.

The bing could have been a very dangerous place, especially for an unattended four-year-old. I can't comprehend how anyone could let their child play next to a large pond out of sight of anyone. And out of earshot, so even if I did scream, nobody would have heard me anyway!

Our 'coal' came from the bing. It was actually just coal dust put into a black bin bag and kept at the front door on the outside landing where water was added to turn it into a brick you could burn.

That was the only form of heating we had, so our bedroom was really cold in the winter. Sarah and I had a 'hot pig', a clay hot water bottle that stayed warm for hours, so that, plus a few coats on top of us, and we wanted for nothing.

When everyone was home from school, we would play at the bing, usually by sliding down the steep shale-like mounds that dotted the area. With the help of a piece of flat wood, we would spend hours going up and down the slopes, all four of us. Free entertainment, I called it.

I still, to this day, love free fun - a walk in the woods is my favourite. You don't see the same thing two days in a row. I'm a wildlife fanatic. I love bird watching, waiting for hours at the outskirts of a badger sett for them and any young to appear. You can usually hear the babies underground, enjoying their play fights that continue above ground. But be careful not to step into their latrine, as they use only one area for everyone to do their 'business.'

Recently, I didn't realise how close to a local sett I was when I stood in a latrine that was five metres square. The smell that suddenly and violently erupted was enough to take the skin off your eyelids. So, what did I do? Took note of the latrine and came back that evening just as it was getting dark, with my son Steven and my sister's boy Kenny, to lay some bait (eg cat food) around the entrances to the sett.

Going by the amount of excavated soil around, you could tell it was from a sett, as it had a red look to it because of the clay deep in the soil that had been brought to the surface, and the entrances were all leaf-free, which meant they must be in use.

My best compliment came from my niece, Sarah's girl.

"I need to thank you, Aunty Maria, for showing me all the great walks in this area. Because I get my stepsons every weekend, I have to find ways to entertain them. It's boring going to the pictures all the time, it takes the fun out of it. So, I've been going to the walks you took me on with your six dogs."

And the two boys loved the woods. Getting dirty was new to them, as they were the cleanest kids you've ever seen, like out of a magazine. It wasn't normal if you ask me.

I still walk around that area to this day and still feel I'm very lucky to live here, surrounded by beautiful scenery. I will never tire of the local landscape; I even get withdrawal symptoms if I'm away for long.

I also walk in 'the perchy', the tip where I got my endless supply of toys and clothes from. I enjoy parking my car, and with a friend, I often take three to four dogs there - but not Scooby Doo, he would chase the deer, and no amount of shouting would get him to give up.

I didn't have the same peace back then as I do now. One summer night Katie decided it was a great idea to get on the very large and impressive white horse that lived in the field behind our block. It didn't go well from the start!

She, drunk as a skunk, talked it over to the fence, with the help of some digestive biscuits. Once there, Katie clambered on top of a fencepost and hurled herself onto the poor horse.

If you know anything about animals, you'll know they have two modes: fight or flight. Well, that white horse took off. Flight was its only mode that day.

After three rounds of the field, Katie was flung off at 50 MPH in the middle of the field, headfirst into the turf. That was another normal day for Katie. There was always some carry-on happening.

Life at Lockview was full of fun, well, in my eyes, it was fun, but I don't think everybody would have called it that. Katie was drinking more than ever; she was never sober, and her self-worth had diminished. From a real looker on her wedding day to this drunk, staggering, fighting, embarrassing state of a mother eleven years later. She was under the constant watch of social workers. She would often leave us all for four or five days at a time with only a loaf of white bread and a bag of white sugar to survive on. Four of us! It's no wonder we were described as 'malnourished' at our medical the day we left Lockview forever.

Dunky would go around our neighbours to ask for food for us. I'm sure they had little enough for their own kids, so why feed four kids who were often abandoned? They must have been sick of helping us because, by that point, it was happening every few weeks. Without warning, she would just take off, without telling anyone where she was going or when she would be back.

It's the most horrible feeling not knowing where your only parent is. I loved Katie to the moon, and the thought of her coming to harm was a huge worry for me. All I ever wanted to do was please her and protect her if I could. I looked after her as best I was able, but I was only little.

No kid that age should have to change their mother's clothes when she is covered in menstrual blood. That was a certainty every month. Sarah and I would have to take off her pants, tights and skirt from her unconscious body, with all of her clothes soaked in blood. Then we would put them into the kitchen sink and try to clean them in cold water, with no washing powder.

No matter how much I tried to create small escapes - whether it was at the bing or exploring the woods - the weight of what was happening at home always found me. Katie's absences left me with a gnawing fear that never went away. I wanted to protect her, even when I couldn't protect myself. And as young as I was, I knew

34

one thing for certain: in Lockview, there were no real breaks coming for us.

Chicken in the Oven

Life didn't give me much warning when things were about to go wrong. It just happened. One minute you're a kid in the park, the next you're left to fend for yourself, and it all goes downhill from there. I was only four, and that day in the swing park with my sister was supposed to be just another day - another day where we were left on our own, another day where our mother, Katie, had somewhere more important to be.

"I need to go home and turn the oven off, got a chicken cooking," she said, like that explained why two kids, one six and one four, were left to look after themselves.

We ended up at the school playground. Hunger crept in, and eventually, I had enough. "I'm going home," I told my sister, hoping she'd come with me.

"On you go," she replied, without much thought.

So, I did.

On the way home, I saw a pair of wheels that I knew I could give my brother for him to make a bogey. So, I went into a gap in the large metal fence to get the wheels for the bogey for my brother.

Those wheels, how was I to know they would nearly cost me my life? On my way for the wheels, I cut my thumb on thorns, and just as that happened, a stranger came to the fence, a man about fifty.

He said, "Come out of there, you might cut yourself."

As I had already cut myself, I ignored him, but he didn't give up.

When I got back to the hole in the fence, he insisted I couldn't go out the way I went in but instead went into the field, to the left. I didn't understand why he said this, so I just went out onto the road the way I came in.

All of a sudden, WHAM! He put me through the barbed wire fence that divided the road and the small field beside it. All I remember is being punched hard by the man who looked like my dad! Then he reached across and lifted a long wood branch and brought it down on my forehead full force.

At that point I must have fallen unconscious. When I came to, I knew I was alone; he wasn't anywhere to be seen. I waited for what felt like hours, and he didn't come back.

So, I decided to take the chance. As I looked up the road, I saw him turn the corner out of sight. I waited another long while before I went home. As I walked along the road covered in my own blood, I came to a gypsy encampment where a man came running up to me but I ran away from him. After what had just happened, I thought he was going to attack me as well.

I ended up running out into the middle of the road, bouncing off the side of a car and right back on to the side of the pavement as the car just kept on going.

The female gypsy shouted at him and said, "Leave the wain alone!" She came over to me and calmed me down, telling me it would be fine and everything was okay. She said the gypsy man was her brother and he was only trying to help me.

I believed the lady and I let the man carry me home, the lady walking beside us.

When we arrived, the man knocked on the door with me in his arms and my mum assumed that he was the one who had knocked me down. She started to attack him!

His sister tried to calm my mum down, telling her that it wasn't him that had done it. After she calmed down, we phoned the police, who came quickly in a van. They took us to the hospital in their van, and on the way there, we saw my sister walking along the road. She had been left alone in the school this whole time!

We had been taught to run away from the police, so when she saw us, she legged it and we had to shout after her that it was alright. She eventually got in the van with us and we all went to Law Hospital together.

There were lots of people were asking me lots of questions at the hospital. It was all a bit of a blur but I do remember I got a lollipop as I was leaving.

On the way back to our house, the policeman told me, "The only reason you're alive is because he thought you were dead."

The attack left me with emotional and physical scars, including a twisted left eye which only got fixed when I was twelve years old.

That day wasn't just about the physical pain - it was the moment I started to realise that life had no safety net. The police may have told me I was lucky to be alive, but the truth was, I felt anything but lucky. It was the first time I understood that no one really cared what happened to a kid like me.

That day, I learned no one was coming to save me. But the scars - both the visible ones and the ones no one sees - are always there, a reminder that life was going to be a fight, and I was on my own in it.

World of Chaos

Katie's world was unpredictable, and before I had started primary school I was dragged along for the ride. From pub to pub, wherever she went, I followed. Life wasn't just about the chaos at home, it was about being part of Katie's world, even when I wished I wasn't. The pubs, the people, the long nights waiting for her to come back, it was all a part of the routine, one I couldn't escape.

During the day when the others were at school, Katie often took me with her on her drinking travels. I could describe all the pubs within a two-mile radius of Lockview. Especially one pub that I'm sure was in Cambusnethan which was a frequent stop-off for Katie and me. One day, she took me into that pub, plonked me down at a side table in the lounge with a can of cola and a bag of plain crisps, saying, "I'll be back soon."

That was a total lie. I could see her from my chair, in the bar throwing herself at any man who she thought would buy her a drink. I was only four, but even I was embarrassed for her.

The pub was a typical one from the 70s, with a lounge that had a carpet your shoes stuck to, circular tables with three or four stools around them, an ashtray in the middle, and four beer mats on the table itself. Nothing special.

The only other people in the lounge that night were a nice old couple in the corner near the walkway to the bar, and a very drunk man. I'm sure I sat there for at least three hours, watching Katie through the small opening at the right-hand end of the bar. I would catch quick glimpses of her hanging over some random man.

She never acknowledged me in the lounge. The drunk man had been in the lounge the entire time I was, at the small gritty table next to the door. But suddenly, he decided he had seen enough of this wee kid, dirty and unkempt, being neglected. In his drunken state, he thought it was a great idea to take me home to his house and save me from the wicked woman.

He approached me, saying, "Come on, kid, you're gonna live with me," and tried to get me out of the pub. Fortunately, the old couple saw it all and jumped to my aid. Within ten seconds, I was in a tug of war, with me being tugged in all directions between the drunk man and the good Samaritans. The old couple won, I'm glad to say.

In the middle of Newmains stands an impressive roundabout with a statue of a soldier at its centre, mounted on a granite plinth. On the front, there's a plaque with two crossed rifles. How do I know so much about that roundabout? Because Katie often left me there while she flitted between The Kilt and The Fourways—two pubs across the road from each other.

She knew I could never get off a busy roundabout with eight exits, so in her deranged mind, it was the perfect place to leave me. I could see her darting between both pubs. Sometimes, she'd bring me a bag of crisps and, if I was very lucky, a can of cola.

I'd spend hours on that roundabout, most of the time trying with all my might to pry those two rifles from the granite plinth. I never did manage it—they're still there to this day. I giggle whenever I pass them and say, *One day, you will be mine.*

My good friend Bangers said, *I'd kick the chin clean off your mum if she was here,* when I happened to tell him this recently.

But the worst part isn't that Katie left her four-year-old there—it's that, facing that roundabout, there's a fucking police station.

43

Food at Lockview was always in very short supply. Drink was much more important than food for growing, hungry children. We didn't have a fridge or a freezer, so there was no point in having food.

One day, I was so hungry that I searched the house for something to kill the hunger pangs. The only thing I found was a dozen or so Brussels sprouts that were, unfortunately, covered in hairy mould. Obviously well past their best, but with nothing else to eat, I removed the outer leaves with the mould and ate what remained.

Because Katie would often leave us to fend for ourselves, Dunky became our saviour scavenging the neighbourhood for food, so we didn't spend the day hungry. Never mind that we were so dirty that we looked like we'd been in a coal mine!

One night, Dunky and a friend were walking past a bungalow in Cambusnethan when, for reasons I can't fathom, they decided to rob it. I remember him coming home that dark, dreary night with his loot, an engagement ring, a large torch that I became the very proud owner of, and an assortment of jewellery. Dunky was only eleven years old, and it was his first burglary. Surely that was the time to chastise him to the hilt, but no, instead Katie made him feel like a hero!

I fell in love with the large red and white torch! But within a few hours, it stopped working because I had depleted the battery, so it got discarded with all the other detritus behind the unit in the corner. Within two days, we had two policemen in our house asking all sorts of questions.

I had my eyes on the black, rubber torch belonging to one of the police men and said to him, "I like your torch, but mine is far better!"

"You have a torch?"

"Aye, wait till I show you," and with that, I leaped like a gazelle into the corner to retrieve my new torch.

The policemen smiled at each other, but Dunky and Katie just glared at me. If Katie hadn't tried to pawn the ring the day after the break-in, Dunky might have gotten away with it.

.oOo.

Starting school was a whole new world, away from the drinking, the unpredictability, and the constant edge that came with living under Katie's rule. School wasn't about survival, dodging punches, or scavenging for food—it was a world where things made sense, where rules were followed, and where I could forget about Lockview for a few hours each day. Of course, that didn't mean I could escape it completely. No matter how much I loved being in school, the weight of home life was always there, waiting. But for the first time, there was a

45

place where things were different, where chaos didn't rule everything.

Stepping into Newmains Primary was like crossing a line from one existence into another, one where things had a rhythm, a structure that had nothing to do with alcohol or survival. My teacher was called Mrs. Park—go figure! I can remember that day like it just happened. Katie walked me up, along with Sarah and Roddy, who went to the same school as I was about to start. I never got to go to nursery school or engage with kids my own age before school, so it was a very big, scary old place to a five-year-old. Katie did take me all the way into my class. Mrs. Park met Mrs. Park—two people who were so opposite. Katie only stayed about five minutes, long enough to see me seated.

One of the other girls was inconsolable, her screams could be heard at John o' Groats. Her mum stayed with her for the whole morning, and we only did a half-day for that week. If her mum was Katie, she wouldn't have gotten away with that carry-on. A quick and severe slap to the back of my head was enough to remind me who was the boss: Katie.

I loved school; it got me into another world where folk were normal and not drunk at every opportunity. However, in order to get to school I had to walk a long way. I was crossing very busy roads and making my own way when I was only five.

I once stole a wooden jigsaw from my classroom, and I really thought Katie would be proud of me, but she totally turned the tables on me and marched me back to school and made me admit my guilt. What a hypocrite. If it didn't suit Katie, it probably didn't happen. She really was the boss. And she let you know that at every opportunity.

School gave me a glimpse of what life could be—a world with rules, where things made sense, and where I wasn't constantly on edge. But it was just that—a glimpse. No matter how much I loved being away from Lockview, the bell would ring, and I'd be back on Overtown Road, walking towards whatever new torment was waiting for me. I always knew, deep down, that school couldn't save me from the life I was living. And soon enough, I'd be thrown right back into the unpredictability that came with living under Katie's roof.

.oOo.

I once found a beauty of a plastic boat—orange and white – whilst searching the tip. At this time Katie was 'out' for a few days. Sarah, Roddy, and I were all sat at the coal fire burning 'portholes' in the boat with the red-hot poker.

"Do you think it's hot, Sarah?"

"Aye, look, it's glowing red."

"What do you say we try it out on Maria's arm?" Roddy said, mischief in his eyes.

"Aye, great idea!" Sarah agreed.

I screamed, "Just look at it! It's red hot!"

As a kid, I used to walk around everywhere with my sleeves up to my elbows. It was like Maria's trademark. The idea of them burning my arms was terrifying.

But they weren't to be deterred. Sarah held my right arm rigid while Roddy put the glowing red-hot metal poker up the length of my arm about nine times. I was screaming for my life, but they didn't care and nobody came to help me.

The next day, Katie came home to see her four-year-old's right arm covered from the wrist to the elbow with large, very angry burn marks. It wasn't a good look. So, Katie bandaged my arm, using a second hand, dry bandage.

She said, "Don't you dare let the teacher see that bandage!"

There was no real taking care of the burns, not a single word of comfort, just Katie making sure that nobody knew what had happened.

That was her only worry—what a selfish cow!

I was a no-bother child, I was never a bother to anyone, just a happy wee kid. But inside, I wasn't that happy wee person; I was ridden with what I now know was 'anxiety.'

One evening Roddy came in with a very badly broken wrist. The bone was nearly sticking out the front of his arm.

"I think I've broken my wrist," he announced to anyone who would listen.

"Nothing wrong with it, go away." Katie replied.

As he hung his limp wrist over the corner of the sideboard it was easy to tell that, of course, there was something wrong with it. Any layperson could see.His injury was 100% evident. But Katie was having none of it. Looking after her child who had a serious injury or having another lager? No contest! Like when it was a toss-up between paying rent to keep a roof over your four kids' heads, or lagers. Always, the lager won.

Eventually, Roddy appeared at the door the proud owner of a plaster cast on his wrist, or a stookie as Scottish folk call it.

"How the fuck did you get that?" Katie asked.

"The woman in the next block took me in an ambulance to hospital, and I was right, it is broken!"

A nurse who lived near us had seen his poorly wrist and told him to go tell Katie.

"I'd done that, but she says it's okay," he told her.

She came to our door, just walked in after yelling and no reply from the door knocks. All she found was a very drunk woman. So the nurse took Roddy home and called an ambulance.

All the injuries and neglect were starting to become obvious and our time at Lockview eventually came to an abrupt end.

The day we left was, to me, just another day, but when we were taken to the doctors, it was my first inkling that something was afoot. The doctor gave Sarah and me a full medical, though we still didn't know what was happening.

At the medical, the doctor said, "Oh my god, you're really skimpy."

When he saw Sarah, he declared, "You're even skimpier."

That became the joke of our family:

"You're skimpy!"

"Well, you're even skimpier!"

After the lunchtime medical, Sarah and I were taken back to Lockview for the very last time although we didn't know it.

Then we got into our social worker's car and drove from Lockview to Lanark to our new foster parents, the

Mclays who turned out to be two of the cruellest folk I ever met.

Leaving Lockview felt like another change in a life full of changes I never had a say in. Even as we were driven away that day, I didn't know how different things would become. Lockview had been full of chaos, but at least it was a chaos I knew. I was used to drinkers and drug addicts around me, not churchgoers like the ones I was now going to live with.

That day we left, Katie had said, "It's only for a week."

How could you watch your four kids go off in cars with social workers and not show any emotion? She didn't give a fuck! That one week turned into eleven long years and those had to be faced without Katie.

Lanark

Leaving Lockview behind didn't mean leaving behind the damage it had done. As we arrived at the Mclays, everything about the place felt alien. It was clean, ordered, and nothing like the life we had known. But behind the neat surfaces, I could already tell that the structures and rules would keep tightening around us, restricting everything we did. We were no longer in chaos, but we were still far from being a real family.

The first shock was that the four of us were separated, Sarah and I went to the foster parents, Dunky Into the Dale House Children's Home in Lanark, and Roddy was left at our granny and grandad's.

We arrived in Lanark around 2pm, and Sarah and I were straining our necks to look out of Wee Streaky's car windows at where we were going. It looked like a lovely town with a country feel, but it was a dreary sort of day. From the moment we got there, I didn't like them.

"Take your shoes off before you come in," the lady said in a no-nonsense tone.

Going from a house with hardly any rules to their house, which had nothing but rules, wasn't an easy transition for us. We had to take our shoes off at the door, so before I was even inside, I had a rule to stick to. Never had I heard such nonsense in my life!

Their names were Charlie and Nan, but we were told we should call them Uncle and Aunty. They were more strangers than parents to a six and eight-year-old.

Once introduced, we were shown their house, a two-bedroom cottage on the grounds of an estate called Ridgepark. The main house is now a residential place for adults with learning difficulties but at the time it was a children's home. Ridgepark House itself was a large, very grand, mansion, with a walled garden and two cottages. It had one cottage at the entrance that served as a gatehouse, and the Mclay's cottage at the other end of the property, which had been converted into a residence.

I was to find out later that Mr Mclay was high up in Lanarkshire social work department. No wonder he was living rent-free in a lovely cottage on a private estate..

As we took in our new surroundings, the one thing that really struck me was how clean the place was; it was immaculate. In the bedroom were two single beds and a chest of drawers, with nothing else. No toys, books, clothes. Nothing.

I could understand having to take my shoes off at the door if the floors were covered in brand-new carpets or flooring, but the carpets looked as old as Charlie and Nan themselves. We soon learned that the house was always tidy because we were never allowed to play inside. Or when we did, it was in the 3ft-by-3ft entrance porch at the front door, a door we never used, also known as a vestibule.

Fuzzy Felt was my favourite toy; I could make any scene I wanted. Mostly it was a farmyard setting and I had all the animals I needed for a farm. I would take it with me and spend hours in that vestibule, where all I had for company was the wind coming from under the front door.

The first weeks at Lanark were filled with doctors' appointments, social worker visits, and buying a whole new wardrobe of clothes. And they had a car! An orange Volkswagen Beetle, one of the first to come out—I know that because Charlie was never done telling anyone who would listen about it.

We had a lovely room at the Mclays', but we were not allowed in it during the day; it was only for sleeping in. We weren't allowed to go to school for about two months because of our depleted state of health. I was so thin and malnourished I had to sleep with a crazy orange fluffy tank top to keep the heat in me. The top reminded me of loft insulation.

Life at the Mclays was so different from Lockview. For example, at the Mclays', we had money to save, a thing we had never experienced before. I had a plastic apple bank, and Sarah had an orange-shaped bank. We had managed to save a bit of money each, it wasn't a lot but it was a huge amount to us.

The Mclays were so different from what we had been living with, the total opposite in every way except for the drinking. That was one constant in my life, but this time it wasn't lagers; it was bottles of whisky. They were what I now know as 'functional alcoholics'.

One day, probably just a few months after we went to Lanark, Katie appeared at the door of the Mclays'. I don't remember too much except I know I was over the moon to see her.

Katie said to me, "Has she checked your head for head lice?"

We all had nits for as long as I can remember. Mind, the "bone comb" was never far away, and if you've never had the pleasure of a bone comb, I will explain how it goes—you get gripped in a vice-like grasp from Katie, usually after a few lagers, so struggling was pointless. Then, with swift downward strokes, she would rip the comb through your hair, hoping to ensnare any unsuspecting wee black nits. She always managed to find a ton of them, but she never managed to get rid of all of them.

Katie didn't stay very long that day, she clearly wasn't welcome. And when she had gone, we realised she had stolen our money banks.

That night I calmly said, "Oh, by the way, Katie says you need to look at my head for lice!"

I announced it without batting an eyelid, and at lightning speed, I was in the bathroom, head over the sink, which by the second was growing blacker and blacker until it was impossible to see the white sink. How Nan hadn't realised we were both infested with head lice is a mystery to me to this day. She must have been horrified when she accessed the extent of the problem. What a mug she must have felt!

Every night, Nan would read a page of the novel, 'Black Beauty' to us in bed. I enjoyed hearing about the happenings of the poor horse, who reminded me of myself—no mother or father around to protect him at his most vulnerable times—and no say in what was to happen to him next—just the same as me.

Social work decided my future from the day we left Katie. No matter what anyone said, if it didn't come out the mouth of your current social worker, it didn't matter.

Apart from reading the book to us every night, Nan was also knitting us both a multi-coloured poncho in a large chunky style, very noticeable. In fact, I'd say you could probably have seen them from space, they were that shockingly bright. We were both in fear of the day we would have to go out in public with them on but fortunately, that day never came.

I soon realised more than a week had passed, so why was I not back with Katie? I was never told the answer; she just drifted into my past like a dream. I never forgot her last words to me at 92A, "We will be together again soon." What a barefaced lie, and she knew it when she was saying it right into her kids' faces. I suppose she knew then that she was free to drink all day every day, which seemed to be her only ambition.

The backseat of Mr Mclay's car was made of PVC and was very, very cold. It didn't smell nice; it had a very chemical smell to it. But that car was his pride and joy. Sometimes he would take us to visit Dunky in the children's home at the opposite end of Lanark after school and we would have our dinner at with Dunky. Then, about 7pm, Charlie's orange Beetle would pick us up again.

I hated the ride back to the Mclays'; the car would be freezing cold, the PVC was even colder, and I knew it wasn't going to heat up any time soon. I'm sure that car came with heating, but I never felt it.

After about three months at the Mclays', we started to go to the local primary school, which was a relief from the boredom of staying in their home. Lanark Primary, it was called, and it was a ¾ mile walk from the Mclays'. We walked there and back every day, no chance of a ride in the orange Beetle. I was very behind at school because I had been absent for most of my first two years, and I never had the opportunity to go to nursery school because we were never in one place long enough, and because Katie was never sober long enough to remember the address of the local nursery or the start date. So, I was far behind the rest of my class, and I struggled at every stage. I did try though.

Having to do our homework every night at the Mclays' was a strange thing for us. There was a jug with pencils in it in the corner in front of you as you came into the sitting room, every pencil sharpened with a penknife Charlie kept in a drawer in the same lace-covered corner table. We would sit there with one of them lurking over us until we were finished to their satisfaction, we had never done homework before, as Katie didn't 'believe' in it for her kids.

Then we would have to sit and watch telly with them not programmes that young kids would enjoy. One weekly programme was 'The World at War', which started with faces on a page, then that page would burn, and another creepy face would appear. That scared the life out of me!

We would sit there for hours together on a couch, not allowed to speak while they both got steadily drunk on whisky. Every night was a carbon copy of the night before.

At least now we were being fed, which you would imagine was a great thing, but it wasn't. Most of the food Nan made was alien to me. I had never seen anything like it in my life. Yorkshire puddings, broccoli, tapioca, the list was endless. So, mealtimes became a battle of wits between me and Nan.

Now, if a kid says she hates a certain food, would you make them eat it? That verges on cruelty in my mind and that's what we had to do every day.

Nan was, however, good at making fresh orange juice; every morning, she would stand and squeeze two oranges on her glass juicer, and we really enjoyed that.

For the first time in our lives, we went to church. It was a good twenty-minute walk from the cottage. They took us the first time to show us where to sit, but after that, we only went by ourselves. We soon figured out that if you sat upstairs at the back, nobody could see what you were doing.

Why are all churches the same inside? Rows of wooden benches, all with their own pile of Bibles, always with a deep red cover. The number of germs on those books must have been chronic. We would be wearing our good clothes - usually a dress or skirts. I hated them; I always felt very vulnerable in a skirt and would take it off as soon as we got home.

The time was drawing near to the day we would have to wear Nan's ugly new knitted ponchos to church.

"Please, God, no!" I thought, and fate stepped in.

Wee Streakie came to tell us that Dunky had found out he would soon be moving to a newly built children's home, five miles away in Carluke.

"Well, so am I," I said sticking out my chin. I was adamant that I was going wherever Dunky was going, and I would have followed him to the moon. I must have put up a good argument because that's what happened.

Nan was not very pleased with us wanting to leave, so much so that she took great delight in taking the two chunky-knit rainbow ponchos and unravelling every stitch in front of us with great gusto.

What she didn't know is that we were over the moon to watch them unravel line by line; I must have had to hide a huge smile, as that would have sent her running for a whiskey.

We didn't stay long after that, but that was fine by me. We went to join Dunky in Dale House at the top end of Lanark before we would all move to Carluke together. Dale House was beside Smyllum orphanage - that's been in the news a lot in the last decades because of the cruelty of the nuns who ran it. They dished it out to those poor kids who didn't have family to turn to, so they could be abused over and over again, and nobody turned a hair. Two nuns got put in jail recently for their part in it all; even thought they were both pensioners.

Leaving the Mclays was another shift, but this time, I was ready. The days of sitting in silence, of ugly ponchos, and strange new food were behind us. We were going with Dunky, going to a place where, no matter what, we would be together. I didn't know what Dale House held for us, but after the Mclays, I was willing to take my chances.

Dale House

Leaving the Mclays behind felt like stepping into a completely different world, once again. Dale House was nothing like the life we had known. It was a place of order, routine, and care in ways we'd never experienced before. But there was something else too - Dale House had its own type of unpredictability. This wasn't just about survival anymore; it was about learning to exist in a place that, for the first time, felt stable.

Dale House was run by the council; it had kids of all ages and great staff to look after us. It even had its own kitchen staff. I remember two of them, Vieann and Rena. At teatime, there would always be a plate of homemade sweat treats, and if you ate your food, you got a cake.

When we arrived at Dale House and entered the front door of the grey brick building, we came into a tiled hallway about twenty feet long. To the left was the Matron's office - a very large room with a very busy red

63

carpet. As you went in, there was a desk where everything happened. This is where we went to get our pocket money each Saturday and the first thing Dunky told us was that we had to save half every week. He was right, of course, and it was great when we all went to Butlin's in Filey and had more spending money than the rest of the kids. Thanks, Dunky!

At the bottom end of the office were about a dozen or so seats arranged in a half-circle around a large rug on the floor where we would watch the TV. To the right was a room the same size as the office, which served as the sitting/playroom, with chairs all along the back wall by the door that led into the dining room. A large square television was in the corner. In front of the front door was a very impressive oak staircase that led up to the two dormitories.

Beside the dormitories there was another empty room which they called 'the playroom'. I was surprised by this as there was nothing to play with inside. It turned out that the reason it was empty was that this was to be our bedroom.

Apparently the Mclays had put us out on short notice, and there had been no beds available at Dale House for us. I assume having influence with the council, Charlie was able to twist some arms and so we were sleeping on a mattress on the floor in the playroom.

That continued until I got ill and a doctor came to see me. "Get that kid off that floor and into a bed," He told the staff.

It turned out I had mumps. I had only been at school for half a day, but when I went back at lunchtime, I was very unwell and was not to go back to school for three months. I did get a proper bed though; they put it into that huge, cold, empty playroom, with only me and Sarah.

When you came to the top of the stairs, to the left was a small bedroom where Linda, the matron, slept. Linda Rafferty, as she was known then, was very young to be a matron. She was a brilliant woman, very kind and she genuinely seemed to care about us all. She married a lovely man called Ian, who was a social worker for the Airdrie area. He has unfortunately passed away now. He had a flat in Motherwell and could change his TV channel by shaking a jar of coins in his hand.

Linda didn't move to Carluke when we did, and we were very saddened by that. However, she did re-appear some years later as a deputy matron at Carluke and is still in my life now, whenever I need her.

The grounds at Dale House were brilliant and had everything I wanted. A field in front had two donkeys that belonged to Smyllum, and the handyman (who lived with his lovely wife down by the rail tracks) looked after them.

As I looked out from the front door of Dale House all I could see were green fields and the occasional tree. And one day I noticed carved into the first tree to the left in that first field, read 'King Dunky '74'. I still visit that tree often and imagine Dunky there, carving his title, proud as punch.

When I walked out of the home and went down the only road to the left, I mostly saw bog lands, with a windbreak of trees at the back. Beyond that, there was the railway, then Lanark Golf Course. Just before the rail line, there was a long field that was a gold mine of golf balls. Every Sunday, two of the boys and I would go to the field with random socks to carry our finds back to the clubhouse to swap for sweets. We also raided the wishing well near the loch, so apart from wet socks full of golf balls, we often had a sock full of wet coins. They must have known what we were up to, but they must have needed the change, as we kept it up until we moved to Carluke.

Behind the home was a large tarmac courtyard, a great space for riding bikes or playing 'wallsy' - a simple game where two people took turns kicking a ball at the wall. We spent a whole summer holiday doing that.

At the top of the courtyard was a classroom for the kids of Smyllum. It was an odd-looking, long building raised on pillars, so you could walk or shelter underneath it. To the left was a single wall of windows from one end to the other. I always thought it gave the place the look of a prison.

We rarely mixed with the kids from Smyllum. I only remember once when we were all playing in the classroom together, but we got caught by a nun and were promptly chucked out.

The cloakroom at Dale House was to the right as we entered through the front door and It housed large gas bottles used in the kitchens. Dunky thought it was a good place for a smoke, and I'm sure it was, if only he had taken the time to put his fag out. After he left the room, the place caught fire. The fire bell sounded and everyone ran out of the home!

That caused a right stooshie; we could have all been killed, every child and the staff too. Dunky wasn't a very good criminal, he always seemed to be found out, and he got in big trouble for that.

Out the back of the kitchen, in the courtyard, was where a large milk urn was delivered every day. It held at least two gallons of the freshest, coldest milk in its aluminium walls, which was ladled out into large aluminium jugs, one for each table. In the dining room,

67

we all sat at our own table in groups of four, each with a member of staff. There was a young boy, Gordon who used to sit at my table. For reasons nobody considered until it was far too late, he couldn't seem to put meat (of any kind) in his mouth. He just couldn't do it, no matter how much we or the staff bribed or coaxed him. He wasn't allowed to leave the table until his plate was cleared and would often be sat there until bedtime.

Poor Gordon would have to sit for hours by himself in the dining room, staring at his plate while we were all out playing. Nobody thought to discover if there was a medical reason for his aversion to meat. Well, it turned out he was very unwell - he had leukaemia and he died in the Southern General in Glasgow at the age of seven. RIP, Gordon McGregor.

Eventually Sarah and I were moved from the playroom into the girls dormitory. In Dale House, we had the boys dormitories to the left, and the girls to the right. The dormitories were the same size as the main office and sitting room. It was just as you would imagine, with two rows of single beds and a small bedside cabinet for each. At the time, we had Candlewick bedspreads, usually pink or blue, depending on your luck, and beneath that were two blankets (the kind you find in a hospital), then the top sheet, so we were kept well-warmed.

At the entrance to the dorm, there was a wall of floor-to-ceiling cupboards that housed all our clothes, shoes, bedclothes, and towels. I'm sure if I had lived there all my life with the people who were there at that time, I would have had a very happy childhood.

My favourite member of staff was a brilliant woman who we called, Old May Meek. She was always full of laughter and seemed genuinely caring. She was a very kind person and would often have me or Charles go and stay with her and her husband Joe for an overnight visit. It was great getting 100% of her attention on those visits. Her two kids, Margaret and Billy - a good-looking guy - had already left home, so we would sleep in their room. May had once told Charles that her walls at home were covered in £5 notes. Why that story came about, I have no idea, but it backfired on her.

May Meek was a stout wee woman who used to keep everything in her bra! If you asked her for a needle and thread, she would pull it out from her boobs. One day I decided to keep my money in my bra like May Meek did, but when I went to get it later, I couldn't find it again. That night when I went to have a shower it all fell out around me. So, I didn't do that again.

One night, when Charles was staying over, he asked, "May, what happened to all your £5 notes you had?"

Quick as a flash, she told him, "I had to use them to pay for Billy's wedding."

That satisfied Charles.

The first time I met May Meek was on my first visit to see Dunky at Dale House. I don't remember this, but May often chuckled about our first meeting. She had seen me sitting in a chair in the corner of the sitting room, by the door from the front hallway.

"Can I take your coat?" she asked.

I was horrified, thinking this stranger was trying to steal my new coat!

"No chance!" I screamed at her at the top of my lungs, and what a fright that poor woman must have got that day - the frail wee kid who looked like she wouldn't say boo to a bee suddenly turned into a cornered tiger, ready to fight to the end for a coat - just one stupid coat.

May went to work at Carluke Home, so she was still in my life after Dale House closed down. She worked there until she retired, and right up until she died, I would go and visit her at her home in Lanark.

I liked all the staff at Dale House, except for a bald-headed bully. He had worked at the local grammar school and was one of Dunky's old teachers – but then he just appeared at Dale House one teatime.

Dunky was not happy when the guy started to work at Dale House as one of the staff. He was a horrible man who liked to assert his dominance at every chance he could. He started all sorts of crazy rules, like making us all say, "Blessings on this meal" before every meal, and then having us join hands and say, "Thank you for that meal", afterwards.

What was that narcissist trying to do? Grooming us is the only way to explain it. You can't tell me it was for our own good; it was only to humiliate us and make us feel like we had to be grateful for his intervention in our lives. Nothing was further from the truth.

He suddenly started making the older boys get up at 6am so they could do twenty laps of the football field near the railway tracks. And there was no let-up if the weather wasn't nice. Even on the most miserable mornings, he would force them out of their beds to do the prescribed laps. I went with them on the first day - it was exciting to me and Charles - but we never went again and were so glad we were too young to have to.

That bastard really did get his jollies seeing others suffer. He was allowed to give young girls a bath, which would not be tolerated nowadays, however this was in 1974 and that man got away with anything he wanted.

I would dread bathtime if he was on shift, as he would always be the one to do it. He was so rough with me when it came to washing between my legs, I was always left sore and stinging from how hard he would rub the soap into me, it was not called for to be that violent. He was a tall, strong man who was abusing me every chance he had. I'm sure I wasn't the only one to get that treatment from him. Beware a wolf in sheep's clothing!

Another character from the Dale House staff was Lee, a nice guy, pretty camp, whose favourite pastime was to empty most of a 200ml bottle of tanning oil onto his bare, flabby torso as quickly as possible while lying on a blanket by the statue of Mary that stood on the grass mound near the front door. I would love to see him again, just to let him see how I turned out, and to see if all that tanning oil had done the trick!

There was also a deputy matron, a mean witch of a woman who never smiled and seemed to look for something to be angry about all day, every day. She was usually found lecturing some poor kid who had crossed her path. She would have been right at home in a concentration camp.

She wore skirts every day, usually tweed style, very stuffy looking with a sensible blouse. She probably wasn't much older than fifty, but she looked and dressed like a pensioner headmistress who had fallen from grace. She had a lovely daughter whom I met once; she was very pretty with long brown hair that had a kink to it from the middle down. She was a very kind and nice person, who would make a good friend unlike her mother, whom folk would run from given the chance.

Finally, the time came near for us to leave Dale House - it was closing down, due to the council selling it - and an air of excitement arose about the place. Everything had to be packed up , we were going to a whole different life. Another adventure!

I treated it like another holiday! My entire time at Dale House had been fun from start to finish.

I wasn't to know that I was about to live in a worse place than I could imagine - Carluke Children's Home – nor that the next chapter of my life would be far darker.

Carluke Children's Home was nothing like I had imagined and it would leave its mark in ways I couldn't have anticipated.

Carluke Children's Home

Carluke Children's Home, I still remember the address and the phone number, 39 Station Road, Carluke and 71996, to this day! It felt like a fresh start and it was a really sunny day when we moved to Carluke from Dale House.

We were all loaded into 'van with square wheels' which is what we called the social work minibus, decked out in the Strathclyde cream and blue paintwork. We stuck out like a sore thumb travelling in that thing. Our normal procedure was to hide under the seats until we were outside the town, so none of our schoolmates saw us.

It was only a twenty-minute drive to the new home, but we treated it like a great day out. We were all so hyped up that none of us could sit down.

The sterile newness of Carluke made it seem like a different world to Dale House. The reality of the place hit us the moment we arrived and it wasn't the freedom we thought it might be.

Immediately, we were greeted by the new matron , a very strict, middle-aged spinster with huge glasses, a tweed skirt and jacket, and a button up blouse. She liked everyone to know that she was in charge, and from the second we got off the square wheeled minibus, she started to show her frightening side.

Matron laid down the new rules to us first. No "Hello kids, it's really lovely to meet you all." There were so many new rules that it was hard to keep up with them.

There were twenty-seven of us children living at Carluke on three separate floors, we called them the top, middle, and bottom flats. One of the rules that Matron come up with was that we had to have our shoes on and fully done up before we left the flat, even when coming down to eat in the dining room. However, we also had to remove our shoes before entering the dining room.

It was not too much of a bother to me, but for Dunky, James, and Ronald, who had thirty-hole Doc Martens, it was a real pain. Lacing and unlacing shoes several times a day just to go upstairs and downstairs.

It was a ridiculous rule but it was her way of showing all of us kids who was the boss.

Soon after we arrived, Matron married the nicest man in the world, Tom and became 'Mrs B' (she would probably would have had us keelhauled if we called her by her first name). Tom worked at Larch Grove, a List D School on the outskirts of Glasgow, and he was not a person to be messed with, he could take the skin off your back with his tongue.

However, even though Tom and Mrs B were tough at work, I started to see a softer side to them both. And being married to Tom seemed to mellow Mrs B quite a bit. Tom and I became real friends, and I would help him wash his car and saw them both outside the home. I was often round their house, sometimes even having dinner with them, and I think they might have had a soft spot for me. Mrs B made sure not to show it in the home though! It got to the point they both talked about fostering me although that was not really something I wanted, as they were still a little too strict for me.

.oOo.

I kept in touch with Tom and Mr B after I left care and often went to their house in Alloa to visit them. But Mrs

77

B got dementia and passed away in a nursing home. Unfortunately, I lost touch with Tom after his wife died, but I often think of him. He was a brilliant guy, and I was fortunate to have them as part of my life for those years.

.oOo.

From the moment we entered the front double wooden doors at Carluke Home, all we could smell was chipboard, just like the smell that hits you in IKEA. At our reunion, we all agreed that IKEA reminded us of that first day at Carluke. The whole home was brand new, from the carpets to the bedcovers, to the toys, everything was brand new. We were told which bedrooms we would have; Sarah, Dunky, and I were given the first three rooms on the middle flat. It was like being back at Butlin's as we put our clothes away in the three-drawer unit that had a mirror and a small stool under the right-hand side next to the small drawers. There was a single bed to the right of the single window that looked out onto the grass that ran all the way around the back of the home to Mrs B's rent-free house that came with the job. Behind the door stood a white wardrobe that housed our school uniforms and other good clothes. Next to that was a sink with a mirror above it and a small light you turned on with a string switch. That was the extent of my new single bedroom, my first-ever room to myself.

Just inside the front doors, was a small hallway. To the left was the playroom and bedrooms, and to the right was the dining room, kitchen, and laundry. The dining room had tables along the outside of the room and a large roller door hatch that led to the kitchen area. We got our food served there, all in a very civilised manner.

The large kitchen had every appliance anyone could every want. We had a toaster grill that could toast thirty slices at a time, and a 'Jackson' machine that sprayed boiling water. In the middle stood a cooker with about ten gas rings, and a huge oven beneath. On the shelf behind the cooker was, to my small mind, the most amazing machine ever invented - a potato peeler! It was just a large orifice with a very rough wall inside it that spun the tatties around at a fast speed to remove the skin.

There were two large walk-in food storage cupboards in the kitchen too, and next to them was a huge fridge, with a freezer about six feet tall beside it. Those food cupboards were soon discovered to hold all sorts of great treats.

Have you ever had half an hour with a catering block of milk chocolate to munch away at? Well, I have, and I can tell you, it's the bomb! God only knows how the cooks reacted when they found their chocolate with a load of teeth marks on it.

Beside the fridge and freezer was the door into the cooks' rest area, a small square room with half a dozen seats where Vieann would rest. She had sleepy sickness, she explained to me one day when I asked her why, the moment she sat down, she would fall into a deep sleep that could only be ended by giving her a good shake.

Once she said to me, "Call me anything, but don't call me down." Which I think is a good saying.

The other main cook in there was Rena, who was likely another alcoholic. I was sure I had left the drunks behind me, but I was very wrong. Rena was not the only one, Betty (another member of staff) always stank of stale drink too.

Once, Betty had to take Charles and I to a dental appointment, then she was supposed to drop us off at our primary schools. However, as we arrived at the gates to Charles's school, Betty spotted a cow in the field across the way. It had a small plastic dart in its rump (the type you would give a four-year-old for Christmas). So she decided it was her life's mission to get the dart out of the cow.

For a good half hour, she chased that poor animal, trying to grab the dart out of its rump, all to no avail. We were encouraging her, of course, eager to stay off school.

Finally, it was clear that the drink was starting to wear off, she quickly became exhausted, gave up on her mission, and returned both of us to school.

When we first arrived at Carluke Children's Home, we were all sorted into our own flats we explored them. ·They each had seven bedrooms and a small kitchen with a Baby Belling cooker, a toaster, and a small steel sink. The sitting room was a large room with a glass-fronted cabinet that housed James Kierney's football trophies and medals. He was a fantastic footballer but was unfortunately tackled hard one day and broke his ankle. It never healed properly, and his chances of playing for the Celtic were scuppered from that terrible day.

Beside the cabinet was a coffee table that housed the phone for that flat. One wall was lined with chairs and the opposite wall had a big TV in a dark brown unit with doors you could close.

'Very fancy!' I thought.

There were two windows on the front wall, then more of the same chairs along the right wall, all the way to the door. And that was it, nothing else.

One of the staff who was also at Lanark was nicknamed Shagerew. She deserved that title. She was proud to tell us about her boyfriend who drove a powerful motorbike and was a married man. She was fucking proud of that fact! We would often stay overnight at her cottage in Newbigging near Lanark. It was sometimes infested with large beetles, who stayed at the circumference of the room - thank God. She always would have sexy underwear out on show when we went to stay, which I'm sure Charles loved!

Shagarew's favourite program was Crossroads. One evening when I was about fourteen, she got up and turned the TV over to Crossroads when it came on, as she did every evening, but I was having none of it. I got up and turned it back to my program. Well, Shagarew was having none of that, so she turned it back. So, I attacked her like a crazy woman and tossed her headfirst over the telly. She landed in a very ungracious heap behind the TV with its fancy doors.

In my mind that was my house, my home, my telly, not hers. She was there to work, not sit and watch TV.

Shagarew was a petite woman, about 40, who took great delight in saying, "Look at Maria's big bum!"

I never had a big rump by any stretch of her crazy mind!

The day we started our new schools, we were all put on the front steps for a picture. I still have that photo to this day, and I love to look at it and remember that happy, worry-free time. It didn't last long, unfortunately for me. Once school started, it all just fell into place. It felt like school, home, tea, play, bed each day.

I was really missing Katie and was still convinced she would appear one day and take us home to Lockview. Why wouldn't she? She had said she would. I felt safe, though, as I had Dunky. I knew he would never let anyone hurt me - but there's more than one way to hurt someone. The constant waiting for Katie and the hope that she would just be coming around the corner one day soon, made every day painful. Every time the doorbell rang, every car that pulled up, every phone call to the flats, my heart would jump in anticipation and would then be dashed again moments later. It was worse than any punch you could have given me and it never went away.

I hated Parents' Day at school. All the other kids had nice, respectable parents there. I usually had some geeky social worker with a Doctor Who scarf on and hair that hadn't been washed since Christ left Crossford. They didn't give a toot about us; it was only a box-ticking time for them. Once a month, they were supposed to visit us, but if you look at my records, you can plainly see that didn't happen.

.oOo.

83

I must have had seven or eight social workers during my time in care. The last one was the biggest waste of space you could find, a man called Ron. He was a big guy who looked like he could fling cows over high walls with no bother. He wasn't a likeable man, and as a social worker, he was crap. One day, when I was 24, I met him and his wife at Asda, in Motherwell.

"Hello, Maria. How are you doing?"

Well, all my years of anger at how he treated me came flooding back that second, and I gave him his character, and I gave him it tight. "How am I doing? You've got a bloody cheek to ask me that, you fucking useless excuse for a man. You didn't give a shit about me when you were paid to, so why the sudden want to know how I am? You didn't want to know me the day you found me in the reception of Wishaw Social Work, and I told you I was homeless. What was it you said? 'Jesus Christ, I canny even get a coffee.' That really helped me! And when I got a flat at only seventeen, you never came near me once to find out how I was doing, not once. You totally abandoned a seventeen year-old to the world. How you took a wage is beyond me." I'm sure I said more, but I eventually felt vindicated, and it felt good.

"Do you think he heard me?" I asked Sarah.

"I think the whole of Asda heard you, hen. But hey, well said."

I could not believe my eyes the next day when I walked into the doctors, and who was standing in the queue I was about to join, but Ron. He saw me enter and turned around so fast, I'm sure he snapped a rib. He probably thought, "OMG, round 2," but I had my say in Asda. I'm a better person than that, so I just stood behind him and said nothing.

.oOo.

At first, Carluke felt like a holiday. The sun was out every day, we had new toys, new clothes, and an abundance of friends. It was good to be so carefree, and we were very well looked after and fed like kings.

Charles and I were still pals, but I could feel it drifting apart. He had made new friends from school who lived in Unitas Crescent, and he had changed from being a sweet wee red-headed kid who wouldn't say boo to a goose to a thug, virtually overnight.

My first taste of his thuggish behaviour was not long after we went to live in Carluke. One evening, we walked down to Unitas Crescent to see our pals, and he had stolen a dozen eggs from the huge box that lived in the walk-in food cupboard in the kitchen. He egged every house all the way down Station Road, a road full of very nice, impressive houses. It just wasn't the guy I knew, and I could tell by his manner that he was enjoying it.

85

Another time, we were walking back to the home after buying juice. As we went down the back street that led to the Well Green, we passed a brand new, swanky car. Black and so shiny you could see yourself in its paintwork but instead of just looking at it, Charles ran a stone along the whole side, and a deep, nasty gouge instantly appeared.

I felt so sorry for the poor owner, I lost the plot with Charles. "Why the hell did you do that, ya rotten bastard?"

He could tell I was not impressed.

After that day, we hardly ever went anywhere together. He was jailbait.

When it came to making money, Charles was very driven. When we went strawberry picking, he always made more than anyone in the field; from the minute he got off the huge open lorry (I'm sure Health and Safety would be all over anyone transporting about fifty teenagers in an open lorry nowadays) till he got back on, he worked his ass off. All you ever saw was the back of his head as he hurled himself on his knees and up the row. He was always far in front of us.

I was sure he would become a millionaire, but I was told by Yvonne, his big sister (who also had bright red hair), that he is an alcoholic now and does nothing but drink all day, every day. He had a hard time dealing with how his mother had treated him. I know myself how easy it is to turn to drink, but I was fortunate, and I didn't let it get a grip on me. Charles wasn't that lucky. He now lives near Glasgow on his own and has a terrible scar across his face from getting slashed with a car key one night out in Glasgow. He was probably being mouthy, knowing him!

Thinking back on my school days I often wonder how Mrs B could be so ridiculously strict with all of us, and what makes it worse is that she seemed to enjoy making our life as hard as she could.

I remember one snowy day, she insisted Linda wear a pair of farmers' black wellies to high school. Linda was having none of it, and a stand-off was going on in the foyer outside the office at 8am, with Mrs B and a fourteen year-old Linda. Eventually, Linda just told her that she wasn't putting them on, "So you can ram your wellies," and she just walked out the front door to school with no breakfast or anything.

Quite often my friends in the home would find foster parents, so in the shake of a shammy they would be gone from your life. It made me wonder about the value of making friends.

Some would come back when it didn't work out, like me and Sarah. We got foster parents, who didn't give a hoot about the kids they supposedly 'rescued', that's how they saw it, and they felt we should be so very grateful. A lot like people who rescue dogs, and think that dog should be so grateful to them, come back to earth with a bang when they suddenly realise that's actually not the case.

We were made go to church every Sunday. For those at primary school, we had to wear our school clothes which seemed uncalled for. How to make the kid from the home stand out: put them in their school clothes at the weekend. I call that cruelty. The church was next to the home, so at least that was good. It was just like the church that Sarah and I were sent to in Lanark, with the same layout, rows of uncomfortable wooden benches, and the very same red Bibles in a neat pile at the start of the small wooden shelf that ran in front of the bench. There was the obligatory pulpit at the front where the minister stood for an hour every Sunday, spouting nothing of interest to any of us in words that we didn't even understand.

I really think the Bible should be written in a way that most folk would be able to understand it. 'Thou shalt' or 'You bloody well better!' Isn't the second one much easier to understand?

And just like the other church, it had an upstairs with seating for about a hundred people, but we were not allowed upstairs. We always sat in the same seats: downstairs, in the section to the right.

Halfway through the service, the begging bowl would be passed around. We each had 2p to add, and we really grudged that 2p going to the dude in the box. After the folk had been stripped of any spare cash (some even put it in a small brown envelope), the children would be ushered into the church hall at the back, through a small door hidden from view by a very lavish dark red curtain. When we saw it reveal the door, we knew the ear-bashing was over, and we went to Sunday school.

Maybe it was just as well that we had our uniforms on. There, we would do arty things, always about the Bible, just another way to brainwash young minds. That's all I saw, and to this day I won't change my mind.

As if an hour of church every week wasn't enough, we had a Bible basher, who would come to the home every Wednesday from 7 pm to 8 pm. That was beyond a joke. Talk about overkill and grooming of young minds, it felt more like a cult than our home. As if the hour wasn't enough, Mr Munn would also have us remember a verse from the Bible that was presented to us on a small shield-shaped piece of card. More brainwashing for us. So that's what 2p gets you, a thin bit of card. Gee, thanks for that, God!

After church, it was time for our main meal of the day. That's how it was in care, because there were no cooks after 4:30 pm, we had dinner at lunchtime. On a Sunday, we still had our school clothes on at dinnertime. One day, Sarah decided she wanted red sauce on her food, so she very vigorously shook the bottle, but she hadn't noticed that the lid was off. So, everyone on our side of the packed dining room got covered in red sauce. All our uniforms had to be washed before the next morning.

That's what you get if you deck kids out in school clothes when they should be wearing jeans.

If you need to be forced into going to church, it stands to reason you're going to take umbrage. I was in a church when all my pals were out playing; I was taken in at 10:30am to get ready and didn't get off the hook 'till after 1pm.

The kids who came from Lanark nearly filled the new home, but there were spare rooms for a few new kids. One of those families were Ann, Linda, Danny, and their bastard bully of a brother. I won't say his surname out of respect for the others.

Danny and I became good friends and even spent a few romantic times during our teenage years. He was a cute, good-looking dude with dark brown hair that was really nice, with a kink to it – not curly and not straight. He had a cute wee nose and a dimple on his chin. He was a good artist and could copy any picture you put in front of him. Once, he did the cover of the Sex Pistols' album, and it was identical to the original.

Ann was, and still is, the most immaculate person you will meet. Her hair was her pride and joy, and it was always gleaming clean. It's only because of Ann that I know about split ends, because she would sit for hours getting rid of any she found. Even her hairbrushes were laid out in a straight line in her drawers, and all her clothes were like something out of a shop: tidy and colour-coordinated, down to her socks.

When she was about fourteen, Ann was allowed to take over the staff flat on the bottom level. We were all very envious. It had a small room with a single bed, a few bits of white chipboard furniture, and a small kitchen with a cooker and a fridge. That was the extent of the white goods; the only other thing in the tiny room was a two-slice toaster. She also had her own bathroom. I would often hang out with her in her flat. I just wish her knack for keeping the place tidy had rubbed off on me, but sadly it wasn't to be.

Still to this day I can't tidy. My garden is immaculate, hardly a weed to be seen. My paths get power-washed every few months, and I can easily spend ten hours in my garden tidying it up but ask me to do two hours of housework and you would be as well asking me to eat the next kitten that crossed my path.

Linda was a lovely girl who hated the fact that she was a bit chunky, and by that, I mean half a stone overweight, not much at all. She would berate herself about it at every opportunity. That's not a nice way to spend your teenage years, hating yourself for something so petty. She once slipped on ice and broke her leg and had to have a stookie put on. I remember her in her bed with a huge cardboard box over her still damp stookie.

Despite the strict routines, the rigid rules, and the constant pressure to fit into a mould we never quite understood, Carluke Children's Home had its moments. For all its order, it never felt like home, and the pull to be somewhere else, somewhere familiar, was always strong. And soon enough, a brief new chapter in my life was about to begin, one that would take me away from Carluke's walls and into the hands of foster parents.

Fostered

Carluke had given us a strange sense of security, but as with everything in my life, it was temporary. The day came when a new path opened up, one that led us to foster parents who seemed too perfect to be real and, as I quickly found out, were anything but.

Our new foster parents saw our photo on a poster! Must have been like a 'pick 'n' mix' for kids. The first time we all met was at a Halloween party at the home. They brought their own two well-polished kids and it looked like they were the perfect family. It was all for show though.

The next week Sarah and I went to live with them full-time. That's not how it's supposed to happen, but they must have been desperate for the cash we would bring in. At the beginning, all was well, but very quickly, the mask fell. We were paraded about the neighbours, bragging about how we were their foster kids now, and

93

letting everyone know what great folk they were – what an absolute joke! It felt like I had no value as a person and my only worth lay in being 'the foster kid'.

He was a staff member in a List D school, a secure unit for teenagers with issues. The reasons the kids were there were mixed: some for skipping school, some for theft, most for violent outbursts because they had never been given any tools to control their internal anger that was simmering every second of every day just beneath the surface like an unexploded volcano. You wouldn't expect a puncture on your car to fix itself, so why do you think it's easy for kids to fix themselves without the right tools and guidance? It's not possible.

The wife was all done up with her huge Dallas-style bright red hair that hung on her like a red Dolly Parton wig. She talked like she was posh, but it was all a show for anyone looking and ready to fall for their pathetic image of a parent. Again, we should be grateful. We were being 'rescued'. Do I think they would have been foster parents if they didn't get paid? Not a chance on this green earth. Their kids both had the same names as the parents (how far up your own arse would you need to be to call your kids after you BOTH?). They were so opposite from us that you couldn't write it. Both had inherited the fire-red hair and the 'I love me' attitude, and they were so well-behaved it made my skin crawl.

It felt very unnatural, the way they were like wee robots. 'Yes sir, no sir, three bags full, sir,' it was like they had been brainwashed, in my eyes, to not think or feel for themselves. They only seemed to do things to please the parents. Ultimately, it all seemed quite sad to me.

They weren't parents, to me they were tyrants. But we were made to feel that we owed them at every turn, and at every turn, they were finding reasons to blame me. It felt like they were never off my case; I was even chastised for stuff I didn't do.

One day, the husband was driving home and saw me walking home. Some school kids were walking on top of the large sandstone wall that ran around the cemetery we passed.

He said, "I was sure you would be one of the people on that wall, I'm bloody shocked you're not, 'cos let's face it! If there's a wrong thing to do, you will do it," so it really didn't matter if I was in the right or not. I was always bad or wicked or cheeky; I could never win with them.

Not long after we arrived, a small black pup mongrel-type also arrived, but we stayed longer than it did, only because we didn't piss on the floor! It was a cute wee black collie-type pup that was called Blackie. Poor wee soul was set up to fail; he was never properly trained and just expected to do everything perfect the first time.

Well, that's never going to happen with a baby pup; you get out of them what you put into them, it's not rocket science. That wee black pup was my only friend in the world, as I had just been ripped away from everything I knew. All my friends were a distant memory by then, and all I felt that I had was that wee, black, lovable pup.

Then, one day a few weeks after he arrived, he was gone.

I'd gotten in from school to be told he was sent away because he kept pissing in the house! I had once again had something I loved torn from me; it was a hard pill to swallow. I was starting to see a pattern in my short life that I really didn't like. *Was life always going to be full of hard-to-cope-with stuff like this?*

I was so sad that night, I just sat silent.

I remember him asking her, "What's wrong with her?"

What's wrong, you dirty, rotten bastard, is that you're a horrible excuse for a guy, who just tore the heart out of a vulnerable eight-year-old foster kid!

It turned out that shit was normal for him, and he got rid of every dog he got. The couple's nickname in the area was 'too posh to Tinto'. We lived in Tinto Crescent, number 55, one of the less sought-after areas of Wishaw, in other words. Most folk there are glad to be there but they always thought they were far too good for Tinto Crescent.

I was dumbfounded by how they matched kids to foster parents. How could they get it so wrong so often? All I wanted was to live with folk out in the Green Belt with an abundance of animals.

My friend Bin was the one to go live on a farm. He lasted two months. He was stealing the guy's tractors and going for a jolly for ten miles around the local roads, chased by the local bobby with blue lights. I would have been like a pig in shit there! I would only have been a help to them, never ever a bother, so what were the social workers thinking? It just shows that what I felt didn't even come into it. I didn't matter; I was only 'Maria the abandoned kid'. I still had no other voice except my own immature one, that not a soul heard anyway. Talk about ripping the heart out of a bairn – and they did it with a smile. Instead, I got placed with people who lived in the most rundown estate in the town.

I remember the night the social worker came to tell us we were going back to the home we had just left a few months prior, and the blank look on both of their 'caring' faces. They couldn't even look me in the eye that night, the cowards!

I was more than happy to be back in Carluke Home because at least I wasn't being judged at every opportunity and chastised for things I had no control over. Like when I was very badly bitten by a pal's

97

Springer Spaniel, and it tore a huge chunk out of my bicep. But when I went to them, all they said (while blood was streaming down my arm) was, "You must have asked for it!"

Sorry, but how the fuck does an eight-year-old deserve to be torn apart by a mad dog? I'm sure if it was one of their own, it would be a whole different story.

I was only a foster kid, with nobody to stand up for me. What better person to abuse? And they did abuse us at every chance. If you were to ask my opinion on foster parents to this day, I'd still say the same: they're only in it for the money.

I've not once said their name, yet that's not because of respect, it's simply because they don't deserve a mention in MY book. One night the wife got a call from the Social Work Department, asking if she would, for one night only, be able to take in a newborn? She jumped at the chance and probably saw pound signs instantly.

That night, the baby arrived, and she showered it in love, like it was her own kid. The next morning, Social Work called to say that they had found a more suitable house for the baby. She begged and pleaded with them to let her keep the newborn, but it wasn't going to happen, as she already had four kids in her care.

"Well, if I can't keep the baby, you can take Sarah and Maria back to the children's home!"

And that's why we ended up back in Carluke home within three days. What a total cow! So much for having our best interests at heart. Now do you understand how I knew they only wanted the money, not the hassle! They said to the social worker that it was because their kids felt resentment because we were there. Aye, go put the shit on your kids' shoulders, you pair of cowards. I've changed schools thirteen times thanks to frivolous folk like them.

.

Carluke Revisited

I was over the moon to be back where I felt I belonged: Carluke Children's Home, 39 Station Road. I loved it there; it was the only place I had lived for any great length of time up until then. My home, once again. And I knew Katie could find me when she came for me, a thought I held onto for all those years, and no social worker would tell me otherwise.

It's a bit of a red neck going back to the class where you had a leaving party the last time you were there, but Mrs Dunlop was a great teacher and made me feel safe at school. She lived at the bottom of Station Road. Her husband was a farmer who let our class come to the farm and explore it - that was a great day!

Later I even made a life out of working with animals, as I worked in kennels and was a zookeeper for a long time. May Meek, one of my favourite people from Dale House, even brought her grandchildren to see my animals at the zoo, and she once came to my house with her grandson to see my three snakes, though May kept her distance.

Life went back to the usual daft rules when I was back in the home. It was like I had never left, and it felt great to be in a place where I felt the safest again. I didn't miss Wishaw for one second; I just had to put it behind me now, but it's never that easy. It would be great if I could box up the shit in my life and put it away, out of sight, but life's not that simple. Though if you could buy one of those boxes, I would pay handsomely for a big one.

There was always a stigma about being in the home; it was like we had a sign above our heads. If I had a pound for every time I've been asked, "Are you out the home?" I wouldn't need to work again. All we wanted was to be normal, like our pals.

I was envious of my friends with their mum and dad and council house. I didn't need a large house with over thirty rooms or a family with their own boat; I just wanted the life my pals had.

One of the younger girls, Lynn, had found a decent family, so it wasn't too much to imagine; but I was kidding myself. Foster parents, like the ones Lynn lived with, were few and far between, unfortunately. She was a lucky lassie to be matched with them, or her life could have been very different. Every one of my pals knew that their family would have had their back if needed.

I had twenty-six in my family but most of them would never have lifted a finger to help me. I was learning the ways of the world fast, too fast. It felt like my life was spinning out of control, and I was holding on by my fingertips.

Very slowly, and painfully, I was also starting to think that Katie wasn't coming back for me.

When I was only ten, another disaster struck. Dunky, at sixteen years old, joined the army and broke my heart. I can still see him leave the home and walk across the car park, out of view within five seconds. It must have been so hard for him, all of it, leaving home, leaving your only kin, walking into that great unknown and having the real world smack you in the face within the space of five seconds.

Losing Dunky was a hundred times harder than losing Katie for me, as I was suddenly on my own. It was a fear even greater than the day The Hump got a hold of me. I had no idea what I would do without him.

Suddenly, I was fresh meat for vultures, and they were on me before Dunky was even on the train. My life became an absolute hell, with my hero brother gone.

Once Dunky was away, I got bullied badly every day until I left at sixteen. It was mainly from one narcissist, whom I mentioned before, the brother of Anne, Linda and Danny. I was the butt of his cruel shit for what felt like every waking second of every day without any let-up. It didn't matter what I was doing or wearing; he would slag me off for things that weren't even true, like, "Ok, buck teeth."

I've never had buck teeth in my life! But that didn't matter. If Dunky had been around, it would never have happened.

I'm certain all the staff, including Mrs B, were scared of the bully. I say that because they never once did anything to stop it from happening; they all saw it, but not one of them ever helped me out. So much for caring for us, their true colours came out then.

One time, the bully rubbed a used condom in my face. We were out playing in the snow one night when he decided it was a great idea to pin me down and smear his cum all over my face. What a horrible, cruel bastard! But could I tell the staff and get any help? Not a hope in hell.

I found out one of the girls living in the home had two abortions because of him. So, God only knows how many others he abused there.

I would never show my feelings to anyone. That gets very hard to keep up when you're young, but you have to. Sarah and I were not very close when we were in the home, and we didn't really become close until she had her first child. I really felt like she didn't like me, because she never had a good word to say to me and kept away from me as much as possible. The only person I had left in the world didn't want me, so I felt as if I was an only child. I would have killed for her and nearly did.

The bully had set her up to get into a fight with a boy in the home called Cat, who was ready to set about her. I was having none of it. I was so angry at the bully for starting this fight that would hurt Sarah, I grabbed a penknife and went off to confront him.

Fortunately for the bully, I only got to the fire door that split the flat, when Gaynor, one of the staff, saw what was happening and spotted the knife in my right hand.

The staff member grabbed me and got the knife off me. It was just as well, because it felt like I would have killed him. I didn't even think of the consequences of stabbing someone to death; at that moment, it didn't matter.

I'm so glad Gaynor stopped me. I've never, since that horrible night, felt the same urge to kill someone.

As you get older, your chance of finding foster parents goes down every day—a fact I was often reminded of.

As if I really needed to be told that my chance of being a normal kid was disappearing.

It felt like they enjoyed letting us know we were indebted to the home, and that we should be grateful for the care we got. You can't, by any stretch of the imagination, call it care, as that would imply they looked after us. No, they put up with us for a wage. How many of them would work there for free, for the love of kids, and to help make our lives the best they could possibly be? You only get one chance at being young.

When the home first opened, we would get all sorts of people we had never seen before walking into the bedroom while we were asleep, or they would appear at the door of the dining room while we were eating, staring at us like we were a freak show. We would often come home at lunchtime and find a strange car parked up, and we just knew it was another nosey bastard. How would they feel if we all came to their gaff, had a look in every cupboard, opened any drawer we wanted, and then made loud remarks about our view of the place, always bringing it down like they did? It's not a normal way of life, and I hope those who visited are ashamed of themselves.

I'm sure almost all the kids felt like they had a chunk missing from their life, because I certainly did. And I was reminded of that daily, in a lot of different ways. If I was going on holiday, it was me and twenty-six others. You were made to feel like a kid in a home; how many families do you know with twenty-seven kids? We really stuck out like a sore thumb in most places we went. They would often take us away on days out in the minibus with square wheels, to random places like Stirling Castle or Lanark Loch, with a few staff to keep us in line.When we went to the loch, I realised it was the same place that Katie had taken us when we lived in Lockview, for a very rare day out.

.oOo.

It was a really hot summer, and everyone seemed to be happy and content with their lot; it felt like I didn't have a care in the world. It was great to be having a special day with my family, like it was a normal, run-of-the-mill thing to do, but Katie soon put a stop to that.

We had arrived early to make use of the whole day, had our picnic, and Katie had her carry-out; surely nothing could go wrong? But it did go wrong that afternoon. As the day got longer, Katie got steadily more drunk, but she was in a great mood, so we were all happy. She took me on the tow boats that you could hire, a small wooden boat painted bright red that could fit two people.

She was doing fine and was full of gusto, but her enthusiasm got the better of her, and for the first of many times, she got the boat stuck in the middle of nowhere. Because of the hot summer, the horrible black goo that usually sits unseen in the water was now very evident. Katie must have liked that bit of the loch, as she got our wee red boat stuck in it four times! So, four times we had to be rescued, and always by the same wee old man, who by the fourth time was about to explode.

"Right, that's it, ya drunk excuse for a mother. Get to fuck off my boat, before I chuck you and your mokit black kid in this loch. Gee the wean a wash if nothing else, and it might sober you up, wi' any luck."

We were dragged all the way to the jetty where the boats were kept by the now-knackered wee man. All the while, Katie said nothing, which I found very strange, as it certainly wasn't normal for her. We were quickly dumped at the side near the car park.

That's when Katie let him have both barrels, "Ya fuckin dirty wee rat, do that to a wean and ruin her whole day. Oot gon, ya bam. I'm gonna get you sacked for this!"

She knew what she was doing, I suddenly understood. If she had started her ranting in the middle of the loch, he probably would have upended our wee red boat right there and dumped two non-swimmers into that loch with a huge smile on his face.

.oOo.

It felt good being back at Lanark Loch; I felt close to Katie, again. But later, once we were back in the home, it brought all those horrible, wicked feelings of abandonment to the surface once again. I had done a great job of forgetting all that detritus, but now, once again, it was back to haunt me.

You can't ever totally forget it. Sure as fate something will remind you at some point every day. Katie had been out of my life for six years by that time, so I was now being honest with myself and admitting that no, she wouldn't be coming to rescue me, not today, not tomorrow, not ever.

I have a grip like a god when it's something I want, and I more than wanted Katie, I needed her. I would forget about changing her bloodied pants, or her leaving me to fend for myself for 3-5 days without even a "cheerio," or walking with Shane in the pitch-black winter nights by myself at age four, to buy her cans. All that stuff didn't matter any more. All that mattered to me was finding Katie, but I just didn't know how. She had vanished from my life completely by then.

For years, whenever we went past houses on trips (like going on a normal coach to see the pantomime in Glasgow), I would look at the houses and picture which one she might be in. She had to be in one, obviously.

It turned out that I was 100% right, in fact, I could see her house from the motorway, if only I had known back then. I still had this crazy thought that she would appear one day, sober and sorted, and ready to love me, but that was only my dream. The chances of it happening were slim and getting slimmer as each day rolled by.

Then I got my third set of foster parents! Surely this time it had to work; surely, please God, make this be the family I will stay with till I'm grown up—and it actually was.

As the days in Carluke passed, the ache from Dunky's absence dulled but never disappeared. I kept going, just as I always had, but something in me shifted. It wasn't until the news came—a new family, a new place, a new chance—that I began to feel a flicker of hope again.

The Adam family - a name that would come to mean something far different than the foster placements of the past. Maybe this time, things would be different. Maybe, for once, I wouldn't be leaving after just a few months. Maybe this could be home.

A Family

The day I found out I was going to live with the Adam family was unexpected and surreal. Having spent years bouncing between placements, I'd learned not to get my hopes up. Still, a small part of me clung to the hope that this time might be different.

The news came on a cold February night, during what seemed like an ordinary dinner with Mr and Mrs B at their house next door to the children's home. I had my suspicions something was brewing when they treated me to a Chinese meal, a rare indulgence. As we ate, Mr B casually asked, "How would you feel about living in, say, Paisley?"

"Yep, fine by me," I replied, unaware that those four words were about to change my life forever.

After the plates were cleared, they finally spilled the truth. This wasn't just dinner, it was a prelude to life-changing news. If I wanted, I could move in with a new foster family in Paisley. And not just any family, the Adam family lived in Castlehead, the best neighbourhood in town, where houses grew grander the higher up the hill you went. Their home, a sprawling thirty-room mansion, even came with its own boat.

I was stunned. *Could this be the stability and love I'd been longing for?* At that moment, I didn't know that my time living with the Adam family would only last four months. But what I also didn't know was that they would leave an indelible mark on my heart, a love that would last a lifetime.

Bit of a shocker, to say the least. I could go from a home to a mansion in a sentence. I'm sure they were # happy for me to have found such a grand place to live, as they really did try - I can't take that away from them ever. I think they had a bit of a soft spot for me. It never brought me any favours, but it did mean I got to hang about with Tom.

When I went to live with the Adam (not Addams, mind) family, I had already told myself it probably wouldn't work out. *Why should it? It had never worked out before.* I'd lost count of the kids I had seen back in care after a failed foster placement. I'm sure even a bookie would have rejected those odds.

I had to try, though, as I knew by that point, this was probably my last chance to be a normal kid. By then I knew Katie was never coming back, though I wondered if she missed her four kids. That thought tortured me. A question I probably would never get the answer to, and I never did, mainly because any reply would be too scary, so I never asked it. A drunk woman is a truth-talker. Ask any drunk!

When the realisation came over me like a second skin that I was on my own, it hurt bad, but there was nothing, jack shit I could do about it. To feel that alone is never a good place to be.

I was taken to Paisley by my new social worker, Liddia. I've no clue what her second name was, but we just called her Liddia Kettle, a slim, verging on anorexic woman, who I'm sure would have snapped if you blew on her. She had long, mousey brown, straggly hair and wore clothes that your granny would be proud of. How she became a social worker, I never could understand. She was better suited to working in a plant shop with things that didn't talk back to her.

So, from the first meal with Black Forest gateau for pudding, I was already of the mindset that it wasn't going to work out. It turned out that I was wrong on that one. I went to live with them when I was twelve. I'm now fifty-seven and was on the phone to Mum only three hours ago, talking about my visit to see Dad, who is now in a home. He took me out of a home; I wish I could do the same for him, I really do.

When I had spent a few weekends in a row at their house, I was suddenly back to being the kid from the home who should be so grateful for this new life. But I couldn't be that person. Deep down, I still wanted to believe Katie was going to appear, sober, with a nice man, and we would all be together and normal. So, this could only be a stopover. I would try to live with it, no matter how alien it was to me.

Dad picked me up after school to take me to theirs, for good this time. A frightening prospect, but I had to act excited in front of everyone. I didn't want to tell them that I was shaking in my shoes. I had to act grateful, too. I was about to leave my house, my friends, my sister, everything was being left behind, and I was going to a whole new life, far away. And the biggest question on my mind was, *'How will Katie find me when she comes looking?'*

So, after my clothes and the bike Dunky got me (my most loved possession) were loaded into the seven-seater car, I left everything I knew and headed to my new life.

I was terrified. I was to share a room with Jane, their daughter, who was horse-mad and had nice posters all over the walls. It's still a family joke how she had to make room for Elvis posters - because I had a lot. My room in the home was so covered in them that you couldn't see any of the walls; every inch was covered with Elvis. Jane wasn't happy about that and still brings it up to this day.

On the second day, we went away on holiday to Lake Windermere, to the biggest, poshest hotel I had ever seen. One day I was in a children's home the next I was in a stately home fit for royals. But the kid from the home was just below the surface.

Jane's hotel room was huge with lovely plush furniture, a huge bed, and pleasant pictures on the walls; not an Elvis poster in sight, though that would soon change. I spotted a 2ft x 2ft poster of Elvis in a red jacket, with his beautiful black, glossy hair and a slight smirk. I had to have it.

Big fancy hotels don't like you putting Elvis posters over their dainty pictures. I found that out when Mum came in to find Elvis smirking down at her. She went tonto on me, and I couldn't see what her problem was. It was only a poster, surely? At that hotel, you had to get your good kit on to go down to dinner. I had never heard anything so ridiculous and couldn't understand it at all. Maybe Mrs B was working there, thinking up daft rules.

My biggest worry by then was that I would be starting a new school soon, a thought that terrified me. I was going to have to explain who I was, where I came from, and answer a million other questions.

I was right, it was as bad as I had imagined, but it only lasted a few days. When their curiosity was satisfied, they left me alone.

I found that school to be very different to any school I had ever been to, and I've changed schools thirteen times. It was very strict, no messing about, they even took PE deadly seriously. Some of the teachers even wore the funky flat headgear and big black cloaks. *How far up your own arse do you need to be, Mr Teacher?*

You would think I should be so happy—I was living in a big fancy house, we had our own boat and went on fancy holidays—but I was still really a kid out of a home, a place I was missing sorely by then. I missed everything I used to have, and was feeling so homesick, it was eating me up.

Every Saturday, I would cycle to the dry dock where the boat was kept on Love Street and help Dad work on it. I really enjoyed it, but as time went on, I started thinking up ways to get to Carluke. I remember thinking I could just cycle down the motorway, and I would be back. I really thought that could happen.

Eventually, I wore Mum down and got her to drop me off for a day in Carluke.

When we drove past the sign that reads 'Carluke', I felt a surge of relief wash over me like a gust of wind. I was so happy that day; it felt great to be back on familiar soil. It was a weekday, and all my pals were in school, so I waited for them at the gates. When I saw them all again, I was the happiest I had been in a very long time.

They asked me all about my new life and told me everything I had missed in the last two months. After lunch, I just tagged along. I knew who the next teacher was—Mrs Dearie (a brilliant wee woman and the best teacher in the whole school). She and I had got on well, so I took my chance.

"Look, Miss! Maria is here!"

She was as happy to see me as I was to see her. She let me stay in the class, and for that, I was touched. She didn't need to, but she showed me kindness that day, which I remembered forever.

I was a bit of a joker in school, always having a carry-on, and poor Mrs Dearie would usually have to put me out into the corridor at some point because of my antics; I wasn't bad, I just enjoyed a joke.

.oOo.

One day, later on in life, I decided to get the one thing done that I had said I would for a very long time: I apologised to Mrs Dearie. I didn't even know her address, but Jill and I set off in my car with a bunch of flowers to find her and we did find her. I knew the village she lived in, so I just drove there and asked the first person I saw, a man out walking his Doberman, if he knew Jane Dearie. I was about twenty feet from her house.

I was so nervous walking up that path; I figured that she probably wouldn't even remember me, but I had to tell her sorry to her face. I knocked on the side door, and a very fit-looking wee woman answered. I asked her, "Are you Mrs Dearie?"

"Yes," she said.

"I'm Maria Park," I told her, expecting her to say, "Who?"

"What a blast from the past!" she did remember me.

"I just want to say sorry to you."

She looked confused. "Why do you need to say sorry to me?"

I explained how bad I felt for making her life a misery for all that time.

"You made my life fun, Maria. You were always joking around; just sometimes you took it too far."

I was able to tell her about meeting her kids and getting to be their teacher when I took animals to their school from the zoo. It felt great to let her know I had turned out well.

.oOo.

Anyway, that visit to Carluke made my mind up: I knew I had to get back, leave Paisley, and return to the home. Yes, I wanted to trade in a huge house for a children's home.

It was not long after my thirteenth birthday that I told my social worker I wanted to go back to the home. I had only been in Paisley since March, and it was now June. She did her utmost to change my mind, but by then, I was certain. I felt bad about it, but for myself, I had to do it. I never wanted to hurt any of them, but I was desperately unhappy by then.

Four months. That's all it lasted. But for the first time, even after all that, I didn't walk away empty-handed. The Adams weren't just another foster family, they stuck. Thirty rooms, a boat, and a life I could barely understand, but somehow, they still felt like home. Walking away was hard, but I had to go. There was something pulling me back to Carluke, like unfinished business. Maybe I was trading a mansion for a children's home, but this time, I was leaving on my terms, and I knew that, somehow, the Adams would still be part of my life.

The day I left was very upsetting for us all, and I felt bad for being the cause of it. My social worker came in her orange Mini with air conditioning through the floor and told me I wasn't going back to Carluke. I was actually going to Downcraig Home in Castlemilk, Glasgow.

It was a real shock; I felt like I had been stabbed in the back by everyone.

They had put me in the worst home available hoping that I would change my mind and go back to the foster family.

.oOo.

Although I couldn't live with the Adam family, I still felt very close to them. I used to get the bus to Paisley and visit them about once a month. I never really felt part of their world, but it was great to visit. It was a safe place where I felt cared for.

Reunions

I thought I'd be going back to Carluke, back to what I knew, but life had other plans. I found myself in Downcraig, in a home I never expected. A new place, new faces. This time, I wasn't carrying that old sense of dread. Maybe, finally, this was a fresh start, a place where I could breathe. But as much as I tried to settle in, there was still a hole in my chest, a question left unanswered: Katie. I had to know, once and for all, where she was.

I found I liked the predictability of a children's home, being back in that situation. I knew where I was and what was expected of me, so it was fine. I fit right in. My bedroom had had three other beds in it, all for teenage girls who were older than me, all ready to happily show me the ropes. My key worker was a redheaded young woman called Vera, and I instantly took to her. She had a nice, easy-going way about her and was a likeable person. I took to Downcraig like a duck to water; that horrible, sad, homesick feeling was gone.

I was only thirteen, but I knew there were things going on there that weren't right. The first thing I noticed was that the husband of the matron, who lived in the free house next to the home, was in the home more often than she was. If I saw that at only thirteen, the staff must have seen it too. Then one night, the husband of one of the staff was watching a film with us, but he had one of the young boys on his lap. I knew for a fact that wasn't allowed, but there it was, happening right in front of all the staff, so don't tell me they knew nothing.

.oOo.

One day, when I was about thirty, I was at home with my pal, and two detectives turned up. "Are you Maria Park, and were you in Downcraig Children's Home?"

It turned out I was right all along, and three of the staff got jailed. It's all in the papers to read, if you want.

.oOo.

I did get back to Carluke again after Downcraig, where I had only stayed for six months, and it felt great to be somewhere safe and familiar. In the home, we never talked to each other about why we were there; it was like an unspoken rule.

One girl, who I'm gonna call Lilly, had watched her dad murder her mum. *How the hell do you ever get over that?* A more gorgeous kid you wouldn't find; she had the loveliest, long, dark-brown, wavy hair, and the cutest little face you could imagine—a stunning-looking girl, but I'm sure her heart felt just as heavy as mine some days. I would love to know how she turned out; bet she did good!

We had a lot of staff changes at Carluke Home; sometimes you would just get to know them, and then poof! They were gone. You eventually just learned to deal with it and to avoid emotional attachments.

I can't tell you how many times I was told by folk at school, "I wish I was in the home!"

I could have given them a bloody good smack across the jaw for that one. *How crazy would you need to be to think like that?* Why would anyone want to spend every waking moment waiting for their mother to come and rescue them? No, pal, I'm not believing that, even for a second. They didn't think about what they were saying.

In my thirty years of rescuing animals, I've come to learn that a lot of cruelty is caused by ignorance. The "I wish I was in the home," kids were simply ignorant of the truth. When you're in care, they can't kick or cuddle you. I would have happily taken a kicking six days a week if it meant I got one cuddle on day seven.

123

My brother Roddy, who had been living with our grandparents, once arranged to visit us at the home in Carluke one Saturday. I stood from 1pm till bedtime at the gate waiting for him, but he never came.

At about 8pm, May Meek came out and explained that if he wasn't there by then, he wasn't coming. A hard thing for May to do, I'm sure, and a lot harder for me to hear. I never found out why he didn't come and just felt he was selfish for leaving me waiting. My son asked about that day recently, and he said that was the saddest thing he was ever told. That was just life for me: one disappointment after another, and nothing I could do about it.

My big brother Dunk, on the other hand, never lost touch, he wrote me letters from all over the world whilst he was in the army and visited me and Sarah often. He remained the best big brother a little sister could ask for. He died recently, sadly, far too young.

After so many disappointments, I still had no Katie in my life, and that continued to bother me greatly. So, I took the bull by the horns and asked my social worker to try and find her. I wasn't very hopeful that she would be found, as it's a big world.

The social worker found her with one phone call.

The day she told me she had an address for Katie, I really felt like I would burst. I wasn't to let Sarah know;

they would tell her at her foster parents' in Overtown (she went to them the same day I went to Paisley).

The only person I told was Mrs Dearie. I could see she was pleased for me, but she also told me to be careful in case I got hurt again. She must have been able to see into the future.

However, it wasn't Katie who wa s about to hurt me, in that instance, but my modern studies teacher. He was a big, lanky bastard who lost his temper with me that day and gave me the kicking of my life.

It was the day that I was due to meet Katie for the first time since she had said she would come to get me within a week. The first time I had seen her since I was six years old. So, to say I was excited might be an understatement - I'm sure I was high as a kite. I won't say I wasn't cheeky to the teacher - I probably was - but that doesn't mean that his reaction was proportionate or fair.

The teacher had put me out of the class, and so I stood looking in the small window of the door, making signs and faces at Linda.

The teacher came charging out like a madman, grabbed me by the neck, lifted me up, and slammed me into a metal fire reel that stood four feet off the ground, just to the left of the stairs. He had me hanging by the throat against it.

125

The geography teacher came through the door at the stairs and I thought that was my kicking over, but I was so wrong. To my horror, the geography teacher just looked at what was happening and turned around.

So the beating continued. I was dragged into a long cupboard and flung full force into a metal filing cabinet at the end wall. I slid down that metal cabinet like a drunk woman. He came at me with every bit of venom he had. He punched the face off me until I was semi-conscious.

The next thing I heard was the same geography teacher shouting, "That's enough, leave her alone."

The modern studies teacher was dragged off me, and by then I was hyperventilating and told to sit at a table. I sat there alone, dripping in blood from my burst eyebrow, all over the small wooden-topped table behind the door of the cupboard.

When the bell went, I shot out of that cupboard to my sister, who was waiting for me at the front steps. I had arranged to meet her as I was going to tell her that I had found Katie.

When I was nearing the front doors, a female English teacher I really liked was just leaving. As I got through the doors, Sarah saw the state of my face and shouted, "What happened to you?"

At that, the English teacher turned around and saw me at the top of the steps, bloodied and bruised, and just turned back and walked away. That was three people I had trusted to help me who let me down in the space of half an hour.

I hoped Katie wasn't about to do the same.

Our social worker was meeting us in the car park and taking Sarah home, while telling her I was going to meet Katie that night. If looks could kill, I would have died in that car that day. Sarah wasn't one bit pleased at the news and glared at me for the entire journey.

At the home, I thought one of the staff would be angry at what had happened to me, dress my wounds, and tell me they would be right up at the school the next day. How much of a fool was I? I was told I probably deserved it. Yes, a fourteen year-old girl deserved a severe kicking from a full-grown man. Come on, guys, wake up and smell the coffee! Do you think the staff would say the same to their kids? Not even in a month of Sundays! (A May Meek saying.)

So, after we dropped Sarah off, we went on to meet Katie in Easterhouse. It was a very quiet journey the whole way. I had so many emotions running through me, I felt like I could explode.

We pulled up to a block of flats in a very uninviting area, full of boarded-up houses and unkempt gardens,

127

with rubbish everywhere. We went up to the second floor and knocked on a grubby door that badly needed painting. Within three seconds, I was standing in front of Katie, my mother. I hadn't seen her since I was six, and I was now fourteen. She hadn't changed one bit.

When she saw the state of my face, she was taken aback but didn't ask. As we sat in her living room with the social worker and Wee Johnny, her current man, I didn't really know the woman I was talking to. She was sober, not falling about drunk, causing fights, or being an embarrassment. I rather liked this Katie.

She eventually asked about my swollen face, and when I told her, she got really angry and demanded to know what was being done about it. I felt twenty feet tall; I had someone in my corner. I knew she would come through. We spent about an hour with them, then left to go back to the home. It was a fast hour, far too fast for me. I was back in the car and heading back when I felt I'd only just got there.

Finding Katie was supposed to change everything. It was supposed to fill the void that had haunted me since childhood, but life rarely follows the script we want.

Even after finding her, the old wounds remained, lingering like ghosts. Now, as I stood on the edge of a new chapter - one I couldn't have imagined - it was time to let go of the past that weighed me down and finally move forward. But could I?

That's the question that lingered as I took one more step into adulthood, carrying the scars of the girl I used to be.

Leaving Care

When I finally left Carluke, it was stepping out into the unknown. No more dormitories or shared bedrooms, no more social workers making decisions for me. For the first time, life was mine to navigate. I wasn't sure what might come next, but I knew one thing for certain: I would never go back to being the scared girl waiting at the gate for someone to rescue me. I was my own person now, free to decide my path, and it felt like a kind of liberation I hadn't known was possible.

I got a job at Glasgow Zoo and working as a zookeeper was the best job I ever had. Being surrounded by so many knowledgeable people, who I could soak up facts about animals from, was the best part. I started as a YTS trainee and was meant to be there for twelve months, but I ended up staying for ten years, eventually becoming a supervisor with five staff under me.

I began in the education department, travelling to schools and colleges with animals, depending on the topic of the lesson. And no, I didn't turn up at a primary school with a tiger on a rope! We took snakes, tarantulas, scorpions, stick insects, and other small creatures. I once returned to my old primary school in Carluke for an ACC (Animal Close Contact) session. It felt incredible to be the teacher for a change—I only wished Mrs Dunlop had been there to see me that day.

I also had the privilege of teaching Mrs Deary's two daughters once. When I later went to see her and express my condolences for a loss, I was able to remind her of that day, and it felt good to say.

My boss at the zoo was the absolute nutty professor—Dr B! Steven St. Clement Bostock, a brilliant man who wrote a book called *Zoos and Animal Rights*. In the introduction, he thanked me personally: *"If it wasn't for Maria doing my work, this book would not be finished."*

I had kept in contact with Katie after that first meeting but she was always drinking and always saying nasty things to me. She called me a bastard and could be incredibly cruel, but I kept thinking, *'if only she could get sober, things would change.'*

Then one day Katie fell in a drunken stupor into a wall. She broke all the bones in her neck. The doctors said that the bones had 'concertinaed'. She was told that first day that she would never move anything except her head again.

And it wasn't looking good for her. I went to the Southern General in Glasgow to see her. I wasn't sure how I felt—confused was the best way to describe it. The thought of losing her made me physically sick; I couldn't keep it down, a reaction that amazed me.

The doctors didn't paint a hopeful picture. They were only ever honest when telling you what had happened and what was about to happen. They told me she would never move anything except her head again—she was now a quadriplegic. That was if she even made it.

They put her into an induced coma to allow her body to recover and to prevent the DTs—delirium tremens. Because she had been a heavy drinker for so long, the DTs were inevitable. She would probably hallucinate, seeing rats running over her or snakes crawling through her hair, among other horrors. So, it was decided that she should be placed in a coma. How fucking jammy was that?

I could understand their thinking, but that didn't mean I had to agree with it. After everything she had done to her four innocent children, the very least she deserved – I thought - was a severe dose of the DTs.

From that day, I started keeping a diary, writing down everything that was happening so Katie could know what she had missed while she was in a coma in high dependency. She enjoyed me reading it to her—I must have read that book to her over twenty times. Writing it helped keep me focused. I knew this was the start of a whole new story for my family.

I was certain this would be the moment I finally got my mum back—the one I wanted. The sober one. The normal one. The one who would love her four kids unconditionally for the rest of their lives, make up for the terrible past she had given us, and finally say how sorry she was.

None of that ever happened.

I'm sure that even if I'd handed her £5 million, she still wouldn't have been able to say sorry. She never once even hinted at an apology.

After she was discharged from high dependency, she was moved to the spinal injuries ward at Edenhall. The staff there were amazing in every way—she got the very best of care in that hospital.

I visited her as often as I could. Once, I even rode my moped to see her. I had to go through the Clyde Tunnel—that was terrifying. I was shitting myself. The noise was deafening, and the speed of the cars rushing past me was frightening. My little 50cc moped could barely manage 35 mph, even on a downhill. I never made that journey on it again.

My life hadn't ironed itself out in the time Katie spent in hospital. If anything, it was worse. I was still getting all the same shit from her every day—no let-up. She must have been thinking up new ways to hurt me every night before she fell asleep.

I was still living by myself in the tower, but I was self-harming, and also drinking. I felt like I had no control over my thoughts. I tried to sort things out in my aching head and heart, but nothing was working. No matter how many questions I had, not one of them had an answer.

One night, in my flat—my so-called safe place—I had got down most of my wee pal, Mrs Vodka, when that old familiar feeling gripped me. The urge to cut myself was strong.

So, I plucked up the courage, talked myself into why it had to happen, and - slash - I cut my right foot. But this was not just a scratch - this was bad. I had cut through a vein, a large one that runs the length of the top of your foot. Blood was shooting up, pooling on my carpet.

As my blood poured from my freshly, severely cut foot, I knew I had gone too far this time. But it was too late. I wasn't in any fit state to go to hospital - I was drunk out of my head on vodka. So, what's the best thing to do? I'm certain it's not 'go to sleep'. But that's exactly what I did.

When I woke the next day, I got the shock of my life. My foot was so swollen it looked like a huge club, covered in dry blood, with an angry-looking vein glaring back at me.

What the hell had I done?

My carpet looked like it had come straight out of a butcher's shop.

I had to go to work at the zoo that day. Long story short, by the end of my shift, my foot had swollen so badly I could hardly walk and I knew I had to get to a hospital.

So, I went back home to the flat and called my friend. I told him some cock-and-bull story about an accident at the elephant enclosure—a place where, funnily enough, I later smashed my index finger. He took me to the hospital, still not having seen my cut.

I was admitted that afternoon and stayed for two nights, finally being discharged on the third day.

That was my wake-up call.

I didn't need to be told twice—I could have died that night because I had cut my foot so badly. I had been incredibly lucky. So, I decided, *that's it with this shit*. And I have never even thought about doing it again, even on my darkest days.

It was clear to me that I needed help. *Professional* help. I wasn't going to be the person to fix my own headspace. I had tried and tried to sort my head out, but now I had to be honest with myself. I needed help. *Desperately.*

I got in touch with my doctor, who put me in contact with a psychiatrist who saved my life. He was a fantastic shrink - he really knew his stuff. Bit by bit, he managed to untangle my horribly messed-up brain. It didn't happen quickly, and for a while, it made my head feel even worse. But slowly, things started coming together.

He explained that by not letting go of the abuse from my past - by keeping it constantly at the front of my mind - *I* was the one allowing them to keep abusing me. *Not them.* They were nowhere to be seen, but they were still hurting me.

It was Maria who was abusing Maria now.

.oOo.

Things changed after that. I had finally found my way into the world, and, surprisingly, it wasn't long before I met someone who changed everything. William wasn't perfect, but we fit together, and for the first time in my young life, I felt like I had a partner, someone who saw me as more than just the girl from the home.

We fell in love, got married, and in what felt like the blink of an eye, I was pregnant. It all happened so quickly, but I was ready for it. Ready to build the kind of life I had never been given. I wasn't going to repeat the past. This was my chance to do things right, to create a family where love and stability were the foundation, not fear and chaos.

Pregnancy brought a joy I never thought possible. It was as if, with every kick, I was reminded that I was moving further and further away from the life Katie had lived. There was no way I was going to be anything like her. I wasn't going to be the mother who abandoned her kids for a drink or left them at the mercy of strangers. No, this child would be loved and cared for, cherished in the way I should have been. I was determined to be the mother that I had never had.

There was no way I was going to be another Katie - the woman who walked into a Social Work Department and demanded they take her four kids off her. When they told her that it didn't work that way, her retort was, "Well, fuck you, I will just dump them outside then," - and she did exactly that. Walked away from four young, scared, starving, nit-ridden kids at the side of the road, just because they were eating up her drink money!

I only found that out by reading my records, so I must have been really young. It was 1970, and I was two and a half, so my abuse had been going on probably since the second I was born, truth be told. I was past all that stuff now; I really was on the road to being a survivor. I never really imagined I could feel as good as I did then. No money in the whole world could buy the happy feeling.

I was a married woman and we had tried for two years to get pregnant, and it was looking like we might never have kids, but then I did a test, and it said 'Positive!'

As per normal, life wasn't about to go like it did for everyone around me. I was about to have to push my shoulders back and start another fight. This time was for my unborn child. I was happy to fight like a Turk for my child, no matter what it would take, this was Maria, no Katie here!

When I went to my doctor to confirm my pregnancy, I took a urine sample which got tested. I had no worries, I had done four tests that weekend, and they were all positive. Happy days. But, just like all my life, things went tits up, and suddenly, I wasn't pregnant anymore. It was like I'd had my legs cut off at the hips. *It couldn't be right, surely?* After more tests at home and the doctor's, I was getting nowhere. One test said 'yes', the other said 'no!'

I got so torn up about it that I eventually called the lab in utter frustration, demanding to know what was going on. I was told by an old woman (or so I thought) that, because of budget cuts, I was being given the cheap tests! *Jesus, Mary, and Joseph, how much more shit would life throw at me?* As if I hadn't been through enough, I was now being denied the chance of competent health care like I wasn't good enough to have that privilege. Fortunately, it all turned out well in the end and I was right: I *was* pregnant! A new chapter of my life was just beginning.

I loved my job at the zoo but I want to concentrate on being a good mother so I left the job when I was pregnant. (My son always jokes, "How many kids can say their mother's job is listed as 'zookeeper' on their birth certificate?")

After leaving Glasgow Zoo, I started rescuing animals. It wasn't uncommon for my kids to find a cage in their bedroom with owl chicks, foxes, hedgehogs, cats, dogs—you name it, they've slept beside it. The fox had to live in my garage; the smell was wicked when it was in the house.

One time, I had to go to the local butcher for cubed beef.

"You having a stew?" he asked.

"No, it's to feed two baby barn owls!"

I'm sure he thought I'd completely lost the plot.

.oOo.

Katie spent two years in hospital recovering, then another two years in a rehabilitation centre, and then she was put into a nursing home in Larkhall. All the time, unable to move. She couldn't even use a wheelchair. Of course, it meant that she was finally sober, but she was a very angry woman and spent the whole eight years wishing she was dead. I had used to blame her behaviour on her drinking but it turned out that she was just as nasty to everyone around her whether she was drunk or not. She was just an angry horrible person. She would still take any opportunity she could to hurt me or make me feel small and unloved.

One morning, as I was getting ready for work, my flat phone rang. It was 7:15 am. The ward sister was calling to tell me they had put Katie on a ventilator during the night. At the time, I didn't fully understand what that meant—I thought 'ventilator' was just another medical term. It was only when I told Frank about the call that I realised the gravity of the situation. A ventilator was just a fancy word for a life support machine.

Frank was a brilliant man, a true friend—genuine in every way. You could go to the ends of the earth and never find a better, kinder man than Frank Mosley.

By that time, I was pregnant with my much-wanted and long-tried-for son, so I had moved back to working at the kennels with Liz and David. Frank lived next door.

He had three dogs, a wife, Ruth, who he absolutely adored, and two grown-up children, Steven and Vicky.

I took to him the moment I met him—he was just that kind of person, the type everyone liked instantly.

I only got to know him because Ruth was in hospital, and he was putting his three dogs in our kennels each day while he went to work. He was an advertising executive and owned the company DMS, handling adverts for all the big newspapers.

The morning I was meant to start helping him, my job was just to do some housework and give Ruth some lunch. I was looking forward to meeting her for the first time but it wasn't to happen. Ruth died the very day I started.

Katie was now in a small ward with five other patients—one of whom was a gangster type from Wishaw who had been shot in the back. His bed was directly across from Katie's, and he was so terrified for his life that he never drew his privacy curtain. Surely that just drew even more attention to him?

Katie had developed a fondness for ginger beer, but she couldn't find any in the hospital shop. I told her I'd get some for her, so I brought her a large plastic bottle of it. The next time I went to visit her, she was like a crazy thing! It turned out, the bottle gave out a loud pop they opened it for her, just as the other patients were all about to go to sleep. The gangster thought he was being ambushed and started screaming like a big kid stuck at the top of a big wheel.

.oOo.

I visited Katie as often as possible, as the nursing home she was not in was only five minutes' drive from my house, but by then Sarah had starting visiting her too. It didn't take Katie long to start playing us one off against the other.

Because of her mobility problems, Katie was entitled to a new car for a member of her family to help her get out and about. At the time, my mode of transport was a blue Fiat 126 - a proper wee bubble car. The only thing you could rely on was that it would break down daily.

However before I could suggest my using Katie's mobility grant to help me get a better car to take her out. It transpired that my sister had a brand new car to add to the two she already had within her household. I never said a word about it, but I could see that being the Katies only support and regular visitor for the past few years meant absolutely nothing to her.

That was when I started to see Katie for the first time, as the real Katie. Not the mother that I wanted her to be, but that she wasn't in any way, shape or form, a nice person. I pretty much stopped going to see her after that

143

My sister and Katie soon fell out at well, and the car was dumped in the nursing home car park about three months after she got it.

New Beginnings

I lived in that flat for eleven years—the longest I'd ever spent in one place—and the only reason I left was because William and I had bought a house, the same house I still live in now. We had looked at a few properties, but the moment I stepped into this one, I knew it was meant for me. It was the exact same layout as my granny and granda's house, and for the first six months, I kept expecting them to walk through the door.

Even after moving, the sound of the buzzer from the multi-storey block stayed with me for years. I told my friend Donna, who lived on the first floor, that I could still hear it, but she didn't quite believe me.

Then one night she was helping me paint the room for my soon-to-be-born son when she suddenly froze. "I heard the buzzer!" she exclaimed.

So, I wasn't off my trolley after all.

It was a *normal* house, a fresh start, a chance to finally have a settled life. Well, as normal as *Mad Maria* would allow. That was the nickname my pals gave me after they found out I spent most Sundays cleaning road signs. Dirty road signs really bugged me.

Dunky, on the other hand, was living in a different place every week, or so it seemed. He had married a lovely girl, Rosemary, who was far too nice for him. By then, he was drinking heavily, and that poor lassie was paying the price. I heard he once locked her in their flat for three days with no food and no phone. I wasn't surprised. Traits of Katie were showing up in him more and more, and when it came to drinking, he was exactly like our mother. He was an alcoholic.

We had that confirmed when he came to Scotland to see Katie after she broke her neck. He was meant to stay with Sarah, and on the morning he arrived, it was barely eight o'clock, but his first thought was having a drink. He sent Kenneth into the kitchen to fetch two wine glasses. Sarah wasn't sure why but gave him the glasses anyway. When she went in to give Dunky a coffee, she found him pouring out two full glasses of wine from - according to Sarah - *"the biggest bottle of wine I've ever seen."*

"Dunky, what are you doing? It's quarter past eight!" she said, horrified.

He barely looked up as he handed her a glass. *"I'm on holiday,"* he replied, as if that explained everything.

How do you argue with thinking like that?

He spent the entire trip out of his head drunk. He went to visit Katie once, saw her lying there in the hospital bed, and never went back.

Sarah had agreed to let him stay with her for the whole holiday, but by the fourth day, she phoned me. *"You need to come and get him,"* she said, sounding beyond fed up. *"I just caught him throwing lit matches at Kenneth."*

That was the final straw.

Wullie went to pick him up, and I could tell he wasn't too pleased about it, but Dunky was my big brother, and as much of a mess as he was, I was still glad to help him when he really needed me. He stayed with us for the rest of his time in Scotland, still drinking every day, but he hardly ate a thing.

One day, he decided to take me out for lunch and told me to pick the place. I drove us to a nice, clean wee pub I knew, a place that did good food. As soon as I parked outside, his whole face changed. It was as if he had just seen his dead granny.

"What the fuck are you doing?" he hissed, sinking lower in his seat.

I frowned, confused. "What's wrong with here?"

He looked around, panic all over his face. *"Do you know how many folk in that Celtic pub want me dead?"*

I didn't ask what he'd done to make enemies that still wanted his guts after twenty years. I just sighed, turned the car around, and drove to a different pub, one where, hopefully, he wasn't top of the most-wanted list.

When the bill came, he pulled out a gold American Express card. I stared at it, stunned. You needed a fair bit of money behind you to get a gold one. I was sure it was stolen, but when I looked closer, I saw his name printed on it. He had a gold American Express card and a weekly benefits book from the nice people at the government—the kind they gave you when you couldn't work. He was on mobility benefit. And yet, he was never done telling us he worked as a cook in a nursing home.

The guy was a joke.

Years later, he let something slip, and I finally found out the truth. He wasn't working as a cook. He was a drug dealer, selling cannabis. He must have been good at it if he had a gold card.

He stayed with us for the rest of that holiday, but by the time I drove him to the bus station, I was more than glad to see him leave. He was hard work.

When our dad died, Dunky came to stay with me again. I was the only mug who would put up with him. This time, he was off the drink, and I was amazed. But eventually, I found myself wishing he'd just take a half and calm down. He did nothing but boss me about, telling me where we were going and when we were going. It wasn't until one night, at my dad's wake, that I finally lost the rag.

We were surrounded by family when Dunky informed me that after this, we were heading to Airdrie to have a coffee with our aunt. That was that. No asking, no discussion. Just *this is what's happening*.

There was no way I was driving halfway across Scotland in the dark just because he had decided we were going. So I told him straight.

He didn't like that.

He got out of my car and slammed my door so hard, I was amazed the window didn't smash.

I drove away, leaving him standing there, outside my dad's house, looking like an abandoned puppy. I'm sure he never thought I'd actually leave him there. But I did. And it felt great.

I went straight to Lanark to collect Steven from the army cadets - the same cadets Dunky had gone to years before. When I got home, Dunky was already back. I didn't even look at him. I just went to bed.

On the day of the funeral, my dad had arranged with the pub owner to have one hundred vodkas and one hundred glasses of whisky lined up on the bar. Anyone who wanted to get out of their head could help themselves. On the way to the airport, Dunky wouldn't shut up about how *everyone* had jumped on those free drinks like their life depended on it.

I thought that if Dunky had still been drinking, he would have been the first one at the bar.

.oOo.

When William and I got married, I didn't invite Katie. There was no way I was going to let her take over *my* big day, and let's be honest - if she had been there, she *would have*. She was that twisted. I did try to involve her in some way, though.

When I first enquired about getting married at New Lanark, the rules had just changed about where you could legally have a wedding. I had no idea what it would cost, so I asked the woman at the desk, and she must have plucked a number out of thin air.

"Em... how does £40 sound?" she said.

"Sounds bloody brilliant! I'll come tomorrow and pay it!" I didn't want to give her time to do her homework and realise the *real* price.

The next day I was going up to New Lanark to pay for the hall, I decided to take Katie with me.

Just getting her into the car was a *challenge* in itself. Her uncooperative, lifeless body might as well have been a sack of bricks, and it took three people and a lot of strength to get her settled.

Before heading off, I had to stop at the shop to get money, and just for a giggle, I picked up a couple of £1 scratch cards - one for me, one for her.

We arrived early, so to pass the time, I pulled out the scratch cards and told Katie to pick one.

She scratched hers—*£20 winner*!

I scratched mine—*£20 winner*!

And just like that, I paid for my wedding with two scratch cards.

Goodbyes

Then, one night at about 8pm, I got a call telling me she was on her way by ambulance, blue lights and siren wailing, to the hospital. She'd had a massive heart attack and a full-blown stroke. As her next of kin they asked me if I wanted her put on a ventilator, a woman who had spent eight years wanting someone to kill her. "No," I said, "she wouldn't want that."

Katie was about to breathe her last, my birth mother was on her deathbed. The person who had brought me into this world, and then abandoned me, was about to leave me for ever. She had never come to save me, and now, finally it sank in that she never would. I sat alone at her bed, watching a nurse pump air into her lungs. I felt so isolated. I was that terrified wee kid again who needed Katie to tell me it would all be fine, but this time, I knew it wasn't going to be.

As I sat watching her take her last breaths, I decided I couldn't do this alone. This was too much, so I called Sarah and explained what was happening. She was there beside me in 15 minutes.

We sat by Katie's bed; the nurse had by then left her alone, and we watched as her breathing grew shallower by the second. It felt so unreal to just sit and watch our mother die. I was beside her, and that was what mattered, although she had abandoned me, I never abandoned her.

As she took her last breath, I was there for her.

.oOo.

I was listed as Katie's next of kin, so I had the job of sorting out her funeral. I did everything by myself, and I felt so confused; it was the end of a long road for me. I wasn't sure how I felt, but I did know that all my unanswered questions would have to stay that way now that the only person who could answer them was gone.

Roddy didn't go to her funeral.

It took me six months to go and pick up her ashes from the funeral home. Every morning, I would say, "Today will be the day," but then I would find ways to get out of it. I just couldn't do it. It felt like it would be *the* end, and you might think I would give a huge sigh of relief at that realisation, but it didn't come.

On the very last day, I knew I just had to do it, so I drove to get her. I was doing fine, or at least I thought I was, but after I drove over the River Clyde, I had to pull over because I was about to be violently sick. I had to put my hazards on and jump out to be sick at the front of my car, a reaction I didn't expect. As I pulled up at the funeral home, I was shaking from head to toe.

You would have thought I was about to enter a cage full of bears with the state I had gotten myself into. I knew what I was going to do once I had her ashes. So, with Katie on the front seat strapped in (I only did that for a giggle), I made my very last trip with her.

They say you should scatter a person's ashes at a place where they spent a lot of time and were happy, but the manager of her local carry-out shop said, "No chance."

I knew where I was going to scatter them, it was a lovely, calm woodland near the banks of the river, a place I walked my dogs often, so I knew if I wanted to, I could be close to her at any time.

I drove straight there, as I just wanted the task over with. The car park and woodland are a five-minute walk away, a walk I didn't want to do with an urn in the crook of my arm, so I drove up the road that led into the woods and parked my car. I took Katie on her last jaunt. I found a lovely beech tree and scattered her ashes around its base. I left the lid buried under it, so I can always know which one was hers.

I only felt calmness the whole time in the woods as I finally said goodbye to the woman who brought me into this world.

After a few minutes, I turned to leave, but just coming through the long wooden gate was what looked like a drag version of Cruella De Vil. Decked out in a long fur coat, she looked like she was on a mission. It did seem strange to be out for a walk in the woods in a fur coat though but who am I to judge?

As we got closer to each other, I could tell she wasn't in the best of moods by the stern look on her plump face. I didn't think much of it though, I just wanted to get rid of the urn I was carrying.

As we got within earshot of each other, she was on my case in an aggressive way, "Is that your car parked down there?"

Before I could say a word, she ranted more.

"Do you know you're not supposed to park there? What exactly were you doing?" Then suddenly her expression softened, her eyes widening when she spotted the purple urn tucked under my arm.

"I was scattering my mother's ashes," I said, keeping my chin up, feeling the weight of the words sink in.

The woman's face turned bright red, and she fumbled over her words, offering a string of apologies as she turned and scurried away, that ridiculous fur coat trailing behind her. Even in death, Katie was still causing me bother but this time, I couldn't help but smile.

As I stood there in the woods, in that strange, quiet moment, I felt something I hadn't expected. Peace. I took one last look at the beech tree and whispered, "I'll give you that one, Katie."

For the first time in my life, it felt like I was no longer carrying her. I walked back to my car, and for once, I wasn't looking over my shoulder.

Endings

Time, they say, can heal all wounds. But I've come to realise that time just piles on the scars, thickening them, making you forget what's underneath until something rips them open again. After I scattered Katie's ashes, I thought I could put the past behind me for good. I'd survived childhood, grown into an adult, built a life, and fought like hell to be everything she wasn't. I had my family, a purpose, and some measure of peace.

For a while, life was normal. I wasn't waiting for the next blow to come, and I wasn't carrying the weight of my past quite as heavily. The nightmare of being abandoned, rejected, and hurt was still there, but buried deeper. I threw myself into raising my children, protecting them from the darkness I had known, and poured my energy into making sure they'd never feel the way I had as a child. It felt like I'd made it through the storm. I'd started to believe that maybe I'd gotten away from it for good.

It turns out, some parts of the past never stay buried. I didn't even know about the Scottish Child Abuse Inquiry - into abuse in care - until a friend casually mentioned it one day, saying, "You should give evidence."

At first, I brushed it off. I'd done enough talking, hadn't I? I'd survived it. *What good would it do to drag all of that up again?*

Once the seed was planted, though, it grew. The more I thought about it, the more I realised that maybe my story wasn't quite done yet. There was still something that needed to be said. So, I made a date to give my evidence to them.

It was a dark, cold day in February, the kind of day you just want to stay in bed. We had a taxi laid on to take my friend Jill and I to The Hilton in Bellshill. The nerves were starting to build, but I wasn't too bad. However, as we entered the very nice hallway, something inside me changed. I felt like I was back in Wee Streakie's car going to the first foster home. I was so very scared and uncertain about how the day would proceed.

In the large room that was hired for the day, we would be away from prying ears, but I was still convinced some of the staff knew why I was there, as if I had a sign round my neck that read 'Abused former children's home inhabitant here'.

There were three other people in the room. Angela, my support person, and two criminal lawyers from Edinburgh. We sat at a long table with cups, plates and coffee for anyone who wanted it. We sat with our backs to the door, with the lawyers to my right and Angela to my left. I was put at ease straight away by the lawyers, which I was so grateful for.

They explained how it would go and what to expect from the day and in the future, and I was told that I could take a break at any time or stop if it got too much. Good to know, but I was doing this in one go. I wasn't putting myself through this again, once was hard enough.

They gently led the questions, starting at the first home I could remember. I spent six hours telling three strangers about the worst parts of my abuse. Bringing it all to the surface was harrowing. I had taken my file from the social work department to let Angela read, and she was amazed there was more information about Katie's rent arrears than about the kids who were being neglected in the house.

To be honest, Angela did look like an easily shocked person, and a lovely lady a hundred times over. However, she still has not returned my hardback copy of 'Lost in Care,' an autobiography by Scotland's 'most feared criminal', James Holland. He is dead now, died from a drug overdose. He was in Carluke Home with me, and I don't know about 'most feared criminal', but I remember him wearing a black donkey jacket, on his knees, crying in pain with toothache in the corner of the playroom in Carluke Home. A toothache can bring down the best!

As the day slowly rolled on, so did my story, but what I didn't realise was every time I said the name of my abusers, Angela would write it down in her notebook. It was my pal who spotted that. We had been told at the start that the police would be informed in case these people still worked with vulnerable kids, so fair enough.

We had lunch, and Jill and I went out for a cigarette, but I could not stop my leg from shaking. It seemed to have a mind of its own.

That was the first thing I noticed was out of my control, but it wasn't to be the last. The afternoon went just like the morning had, but it felt more intense now. That was just tough. I couldn't back out now, and it wouldn't have made much difference anyway since the damage was done, and I was the one who had instigated it.

I just kept telling myself that by giving my evidence, it could stop another kid going through the same or worse. That was certainly true, and it was the only reason I was putting myself through this stuff that I'd kept buried for a very long time at the bottom of a deep hole. I'm really hoping that after this book and my time with Redress Scotland is over, I can have it all put back into that hole; and this time, it's getting capped with a heavy slab. I need to own my life and enjoy what being happy feels like, surely that's not too much to ask for?

By the end of the day of giving evidence, I was drained. I'd spoken for six hours about the worst bits of my life to three strangers and my best pal. I had named all my abusers and Angela had taken their names to be investigated. I, on the other hand, just wanted to be back in a taxi heading to my normal life, where that large hole would be waiting for me. Life went on as normal for everyone else, but not for me. I could feel the black darkness coming back for me, to do with me what it liked again.

The next day, I heard what had happened to the boy in Carluke who had bullied and abused everyone around him and especially me. I had given his name as one of my abusers and it turned out I was not alone.

I had known that the boy didn't get any better as he got older, in fact he turned into a monster rather than a man. I was already aware of one woman that he battered, as she and I were friends. He nearly killed her and did time in jail for that attack. Her bedside cabinet still has a chunk out of the corner, which she told me broke when he smashed her face off it during the assault.

.oOo.

When I had got home from giving evidence to the Inquiry, my mind was like mush; I could not sort anything into any kind of box, no matter how much I wanted to. Instead of making me feel unburdened, it had left me as confused as before. I knew I wasn't going to cope well with it; I could just tell.

If you had told me with your hand on a stack of red-covered Bibles that it was going to mess with my head so much, I would have told you, "Away and behave yourself."

Looking back now, I can see how far I've come. From the terrified, bruised little girl who longed for her mother's love, to the woman who finally found her own strength. I gave evidence, I told my truth, and I reclaimed a part of myself that had been taken away all those years ago. But the fight isn't over. It never really will be. I'll always carry the scars, some on the outside, but most on the inside.

I've learned to make peace with the fact that not everything will heal. I'll always have that fear in me when a stranger passes too close, that instinct to protect what's mine, that memory of dark days. I also know now that those memories don't control me anymore. They're part of who I am, but they don't define me.

I've faced the past head-on, and I'm still standing. I've lived through the worst, and somehow, I've built something good from it.

I met William when I was 17 years old and we have been together now for 40 years. We have had a son and a daughter together and I've raised my children with love, with the care I never had. I've rescued more animals than I can count, offering them the safety and kindness that was denied to me. And with each day that passes, I remind myself that I deserve to be here. I deserve to be happy.

So, to everyone who tried to break me, the foster parents who wanted a payday, the social workers who turned a blind eye, and to the teachers who let me bleed, you didn't win. I did.

This is my story, my life. I made it mine. And now, with the ink of my greyhound tattoo reminding me of every step I've taken, I can finally say, "This is the beginning of the rest of my life."

Printed in Dunstable, United Kingdom